BECOMING DADS

BECOMING DADS

An Innovative Fatherhood Curriculum

FACILITATOR GUIDE

Becoming Dads: An Innovative Fatherhood Curriculum (Facilitator Guide)
First Edition Trade Book, © 2021
© 2021 by Marvin Charles

All rights reserved. No part of this publication may be reproduced, stored in a retrieval system, or transmitted in any form by any means—electronic, mechanical, photocopy, recording, or otherwise—except for brief quotations in critical reviews or articles, without the prior permission of the author or publisher, except as provided by U.S. copyright law.

To contact, or to order additional books:
www.aboutdads.org

Also available on Amazon.com

ISBN: 978-1-952943-99-7

Editorial and Book Packaging: Inspira Literary Solutions, Gig Harbor, WA

Printed in the U.S.A.

Table of Contents

Divine Alternatives for Dads Services ix
Author and Instructor ix

0.0 | Course Introduction 1
0.1 Course Goal 1
0.2 Course Objectives 1
0.3 DADS Pre-survey 2

1.0 | Turning Your Life Around 5
1.1 Engage: The Role of a Dad 6
1.2 The Becoming Dads Pledge 9
1.3 The Dollar Bill Story 11
1.4 This Is Your Life 14
1.6 Change 16
1.7 The Dad Plan 21

2.0 | Every Dad's Challenge: Being There 23
2.1 FatherLESSness 24
2.1. A Want Ad for a Dad... 24
    2.1.b Defining Fatherlessness 25
    2.1.c The Impact of Fatherlessness 28
2.2 FatherFULLness 30
    2.2.a What Children Say about FatherFULLness 31
    2.2.b How Research Defines FatherFULLness 32
    2.2.c What Research Says about FatherFULLness........... 33
2.3 A Lifetime Commitment as a Father 34
    2.3.a The Amos Story 35
    2.3.b What Being Your Child's Father Means to You........ 37
2.4 The Dad Plan... 38

3.0 | What Men Do 41
3.1 Man Up 42
- 3.1.a Activity: What Kind of Man Are You? 43
- 3.1.b The Elephant in the Room 45
- 3.1.c What Do Men Do? 47

3.2 Marry Up 50
- 3.2a Your History with Women 52
- 3.2.b How to Treat a Woman 57

3.3 Daddy Up 61
- 3.3.a What Your Child needs 62
- 3.3.b What Dads Do 67

3.4 The Dad Plan 68

4.0 | Overcoming Challenges 71
4.1 Stable in Stress 72
- 4.1.a The Stress Test 72
- 4.1.b What Is Stress? 73
- 4.1.c The Impact of Stress 75

4.2 The Trouble with Trauma 79
- 4.2.a Cuts Like a Knife 79
- 4.2.a The ACE Study 81
- 4.2.b The Ace Survey 83

4.3 Healing, Forgiving, Making Amends, and Moving On 87
- 4.3.a Dice Activity: 2 Steps Forward, 3 Steps Back 87
- 4.3.b Feel Like Giving Up? 88
- 4.3.c Forgiveness and Moving Forward 91

4.4 The Dad Plan 95

5.0 | Becoming Dad 97
5.1 Better Relational Skills 98
- 5.1.a The Family Tree 98
- 5.1.b Family Needs 99
- 5.1.c Speaking 102
- 5.1.d Listening 104

5.2 Co-Parenting 106
- 5.2.a Family Sculpturing 107

    5.2.b Getting Past the Drama 108
    5.2.c Co-parenting Tips 109
5.3 Better Dad Skills 110
    5.3.a Investing Your Time 110
    5.3.b Leading and Role Modeling 110
    5.3.c Caring for Your Child 112
5.4 The Dad Plan 114

6.0 | Moving Forward 117

6.1 Child Support 118
    6.1.a Activity: Aircraft Carrier Support 118
    6.1.b How DADS Can Help 119
    6.1.c Frequently Asked Questions 121
6.2 Employment 125
    6.2.a Activity: 30 Second Commercial 126
    6.2.b Soft Skills 127
    6.2.c Preparing for Employment 130
6.3 Addictions 134
6.3 Activity: Paper Football Game 134
    6.3a Substance Use Disorder 135
    6.3b Preparing to Change 139
    6.3c Step Up to Change 141
6.4 The Dad Plan 144

7.0 | References 147

Divine Alternatives for Dads Services

Marvin Charles is the founder and executive director of Divine Alternatives for Dads Services based in Seattle, Washington. For over 20 years, he has been effectively helping men in surrounding communities reclaim their positive role as the fathers their children need. Marvin's own powerful story of separation and reunification with his family, parents and children, fueled his passion for ministry, gave him experience, and earned the trust of other men to be their mentor and advisor.

Marvin is also an emerging national leader in creating stronger fathers and healthier families. He travels across the U.S. to speak about empowering fathers, to learn from other national leaders, and to share his successes with other organizations planning to implement fatherhood programs.

Marvin is the author of *Becoming Dads*, which chronicles his life and the beginnings of Divine Alternatives for Dads Services. He is an ordained minister and his extraordinary effectiveness comes from his ability to see through the pain and threats of those he counsels to the powerful change possible by embracing a living God and larger purpose. Neither class nor ethnicity pose an obstacle to Marvin being heard.

Marvin and his wife, Jeanett, have a beautiful blended family of eight children, including Dontay, Nick, Marvin Jr., Jeffrey, Lyric, Devotion, Marvette, and Jamie.

Author and Instructor

George R. Williams, Ph.D., is a trained marriage and family therapist and family life education consultant with almost two decades of experience as a curricula developer, fathering practitioner, master trainer, public speaker and consultant who has passionately served some of our most vulnerable citizens from all walks of life.

Dr. Williams is the Assistant Director for Faith-based and Community Initiatives for the Kansas Department for Children and Families, leading work on state-wide projects such as Mental Health Awareness, Kansas Strong Dads, Social Worker

Courses, the Kansas Community Leadership Enterprise and the Governor's Mental Health Taskforce. Prior to this, he served as the Director of Addiction and Prevention Services, responsible for all Kansas Substance Use Disorder (SUD) services—managing a staff of 23, a budget of $46 million, and oversight of 200 SUD service providers.

Dr. Williams served a decade at the National Center for Fathering as the former executive director of urban fathering developing and delivering fathering education and programming in communities across the country. As a nationally recognized fathering and family expert he has spoken and taught at national conferences including the National PTA Conference, the National Welfare Reform Conference and the National Head Start Fathering Conference and has inspired and helped thousands across the country with his creative, engaging and passionate presentations and training. Dr. Williams has been featured in national media and has authored numerous fathering articles and teaching materials, including *Kansas Strong Dads*, *Super Kids*, *READ to Kids*, *Males to MEN*, *Quenching the Father Thirst*, and *Kansas HOPE Mentoring*. He is a contributing author for the book, *Why Fathers Count*.

Dr. Williams earned his Bachelor of Science degree in computer science and a Doctorate in family studies from Kansas State University (Manhattan, KS.) He earned his Master of Science degree from Friends University (Wichita, KS) in marriage and family therapy. He and Trudy, his wife of thirty-two years, have three sons and a daughter and live in the greater Kansas City area.

0.0 Course Introduction

> Total course time is 6 hours. All listed times are in minutes.
> remaining course time (rct) **360**
> remaining section time (rst) **50**
> estimated section time (est) **5**
> participant page **x**
>
> [Introduce yourself; share what is important for them to know about you.]
>
> **Note:** Frequently remind participants what page you are on. There are other facilitation notes in the Appendix of this manual.

0.1 Course Goal

The goal of the *Becoming Dads* curriculum is to help men in challenging situations to take increasing responsibility and action to heal and make changes necessary to become the dad their children need, so that their children can thrive and be successful for the next generation.

0.2 Course Objectives

> rct 355 | rst 55 | est 5 | page 7
>
> [Read the following]

The purpose of this curriculum is for participants to build knowledge, adjust attitudes, and apply skills related to men becoming the dads their children need. At the completion of the curriculum they will:

1. Face the truth of their past and have hope for a better future
2. Understand the impact in their role as a father
3. Know what their children need from them
4. Be committed to their children for a lifetime
5. Understand the character of a man who lives for others
6. Know how to have a healthy relationship with their child's mother
7. Start on the road to healing and getting past hurdles to effective fathering
8. Have grounding in their spiritual walk and maintenance
9. Improve their employment situation
10. Understand the child support system
11. Get on track to providing child support

---

rct 350 | rst 50 | est 10 | page 8

State: *Next, we will take the DADS pre-survey to measure your fathering attitudes and actions.*

Instruct: *Please take the next five minutes to read the statement and check the box that most closely reflects your answer. The scale is from 1 (strongly disagree) to 5 (strongly agree).*

[Give a one-minute warning when you are ready to resume.]

0.3 DADS Pre-survey

Instructions: *Where indicated please check the box of your response.*

	5 = Strongly Agree	4 = Agree	3 = Neutral	2 = Disagree	1 = Strongly Disagree
1. I would not mind if my son grew up to be someone just like me.	❏	❏	❏	❏	❏

	5 = Strongly Agree	4 = Agree	3 = Neutral	2 = Disagree	1 = Strongly Disagree
2. I want my daughter to marry someone like me.	❏	❏	❏	❏	❏
3. I believe that fathers are just as important as mothers.	❏	❏	❏	❏	❏
4. A father's involvement includes physical, social, emotional, and spiritual presence.	❏	❏	❏	❏	❏
5. I believe that men need help to become the fathers their children need.	❏	❏	❏	❏	❏
6. Men and women should be treated as equals in every way.	❏	❏	❏	❏	❏
7. Fathers and mothers must work together for the benefit of their child even if they are not together.	❏	❏	❏	❏	❏
8. Violence has no place in the family between mothers, fathers, and children.	❏	❏	❏	❏	❏
9. I have open communication with the mother of my child.	❏	❏	❏	❏	❏
10. My child knows that I am available for them night or day.	❏	❏	❏	❏	❏
11. I am responsible to take care of the physical, emotional, social, and spiritual needs of my child.	❏	❏	❏	❏	❏
12. I know where my child should be developmentally.	❏	❏	❏	❏	❏
13. I regularly express my love to my child by saying it and showing it.	❏	❏	❏	❏	❏

	5 = Strongly Agree	4 = Agree	3 = Neutral	2 = Disagree	1 = Strongly Disagree
14. I have regular interaction with my child either by reading, playing, or talking.	❏	❏	❏	❏	❏
15. I am involved in my child's education.	❏	❏	❏	❏	❏
16. I am currently paying child support.	❏	❏	❏	❏	❏
17. I am employed or currently looking for employment.	❏	❏	❏	❏	❏
18. I have regular access to my child anytime during the day.	❏	❏	❏	❏	❏
19. I have started a college saving account for my child and am contributing monthly.	❏	❏	❏	❏	❏
20. I am attending a weekly support group to improve my fathering, spiritual well-being, or sobriety.	❏	❏	❏	❏	❏
21. During my childhood, my parents were always in my life.	❏	❏	❏	❏	❏
22. I have never been incarcerated.	❏	❏	❏	❏	❏
23. I was never abused during my childhood.	❏	❏	❏	❏	❏
24. I have been sober for more than one year.	❏	❏	❏	❏	❏
25. No one in my family has a mental disorder.	❏	❏	❏	❏	❏

Ask: *Does anyone have any questions or comments about the survey?*

1.0 Turning Your Life Around

> rct 340 | rst 40 | est 10 | page 11
>
> [Read the following]

GOAL

To become a better dad
To turn my life around
To face the truth and break free from the things that at one time held me down

OBJECTIVES

1. The Role of a Dad
2. The Dollar Bill Story
3. Are You Ready for a Change?

How widespread is father absence? A past quote from the *New York Times* (1971) says it all, "Most American children suffer too much mother and too little father." In other words, children are missing out on the full benefits of a healthy involved father. Father absence has been at an historic high in America since the 1990s and continues to impact over 25% of U.S. children.

Fathers are critically important to children, as they are their champions and super heroes. Children want and need their fathers. "Nothing can replace a father spending time with his children." Let this be the motivation for fathers to turn their lives around and become the fathers their children need.

1.1 Engage: The Role of a Dad

> **State:** *In our first activity, we are going to take you back to your youth when you use to make things out of paper for fun.*
>
> **Instruct:** *Using a single sheet of paper, you have two minutes to make something out of the paper.*
>
> **Note:** If someone asks what you made, simply reply, "I made something out of the piece of paper."
>
> **State:** *Ready, begin.*
>
> [Give them a one-minute warning when the time is up]

Using a single sheet of paper, you can create many objects. The Japanese culture has an art form called *origami* or "the art of paper folding." There is a good chance when you were in school, you made things to play and sometimes to pass the time. This next exercise may take you back to an early time when you created things with paper for fun.

Instructions: You will be handed a standard 8.5 x 11 sheet of paper. You will be given a time limit in which you will be asked to make something out of that piece of paper. (Williams, 2010)

> [Once the time is up, read the following]
>
> **State:** *The time is up. I would like everyone to show what they made, share what it is, and why they made it.*
>
> [Ask next two questions.]

Process Questions

1. What did you make?
2. Why did you make it?
3. How can you compare this exercise with how you came to be the person you are today?

> **Note:** The following is a list of comparisons of the exercise to fatherhood that the dads might share. Give them time to answer, but if they get stuck you can make the following points:
>
> 1. You were given a piece of paper to shape; fathers are given a baby to shape.
> 2. You were given two minutes; fathers are given 18 years.
> 3. You were given poor instructions; fathers are given no instruction.
> 4. You each made something different; fathers all father differently.
> 5. You made what you knew how; fathers do the best they know how.
> 6. You did not have a model; many fathers did not have a father model.
> 7. You may have done nothing with the paper; many fathers are not involved with their children.
>
> [Ask the following questions.]

   4. What is the implication of this exercise for us?

> **Note:** You have the option of playing hangman to guess the following phrase that summarizes this activity.
>
> [Read the instructions.]

Instructions: Try to choose letters that complete the phrase below that summarizes our previous paper activity.

D								
A								
D								
S								!

(Williams, 2010)

> [Share the correct answer.]
>
> **State:** *Dads are destiny shapers. They don't set the destiny, but shape it.*
>
> **State:** *Dads play a critical role in helping or hindering the success of their child.*
>
> **Transition:** *Next, we will take a closer look at what this course is about.*

1.1 Dads play a critical role in helping or hindering the success of their child.

1.2 The Becoming Dads Pledge

> rct 330 | rst 30 | est 5 | page 13
>
> **State:** *This curriculum is all about becoming better dads, which is something any dad would find useful. The Becoming Dads Pledge is a road map to this curriculum that summarizes the main purpose of each section.*
>
> **Note:** *Be mindful that some may not know how to read.*
>
> **Instruct:** *We are going to read through the following pledge and discuss the questions. I will give you two minutes to read through the pledge yourself and then we will read it together.*
>
> [Wait two minutes, give a time warning.]

For any worthwhile pursuit in life, it is helpful to have a guide that will keep you on the road to success. The following is the "Becoming a Better Dad Pledge," which is a road map to this curriculum. This makes a brief statement about each one of the six sessions.

Please keep in mind that the time you spend in this class is a direct investment in your child. As we become better men, our children benefit from a better dad.

Instructions: Read through the following pledge and answer the process questions. Be ready to discuss with the group.

> **State:** *Let's read the pledge together.*

Becoming a Better Dad

To become a better dad,
I will turn my life around,
face the truth, and break free from the things
that at one time held me down.

To become a better dad,
I will commit to being there
for the sake of my child
by investing this time here.

To become a better dad,
I will do what men do:
mature, respect women, love and serve others.
And that includes my children too.

To become a better dad,
I need healing from my past—
all the hurt, trauma, and failures—
forgiving, making amends, moving forward at last.

To become a better dad,
I will be humble and seek to learn
ways to improve as a parent, co-parent, and citizen,
and let this passion to be better burn.

I will become a better dad,
no matter how tough, I won't quit or give up,
through the support of my faith, family, and community,
until my last breath and my eyes finally shut.

[Read the process questions and give participants time to answer the questions.]

Process Questions

1. Is there anything you would add, delete, or change in this pledge?
2. What is one thing in this pledge that spoke to you?
3. Is this a reasonable goal for your role as a man and father?
4. What might be some challenges to fulfilling this pledge?
5. Would you commit to fulfilling this pledge for your child?

[Summarize the answers.]

State: *This curriculum is about making a commitment to be the dad your child needs, and to make and live the statement that, "I will daddy up!"*

Transition: *Next, we will see that it is not easy being a dad.*

1.2 I will "daddy up."

1.3 The Dollar Bill Story

rct 325 | rst 25 | est 10 | page 14

[Use a dollar bill as a visual aid.]

[Read the following.]

Unfortunately, the role of the father often gets boiled down to one thing: providing. It is like every father in America has the same first name and last name. The first name is Dollar and the last name is Bill. Of course, a large part of being a father is providing, but it's not just about the money.

Additionally, children need the love, support, and guidance from their mothers *and* fathers to help them thrive and be successful in life. Following is the story of a man and father whose first name is Bill and his struggle to be a better father.

The Dollar Bill Story

After serving four years in prison on drug-related charges, William Haynes was lucky to find employment as a sheet metal worker. At 34, the father of five children had never held a job and it felt good to be earning his own money for the first time. But what Haynes didn't know is that child support obligations, which he said he never knew about, had been accruing even while he was incarcerated.

By the time he was released from prison in 2001, he owed $133,000. And, after he was two months or so into the job, the state had started to garnish his pay. "They were taking practically all the money I was making," Haynes said. "I was left with maybe $75 a week. I felt like I was paying a note to a house I would never live in." It was around that time that Haynes met Marvin Charles, who had traveled a similar path in life.

Marvin and his wife, Jeanett, took what they learned working with guys like Haynes, as well as working to win their own children back from the state, to create an organization that helps fathers—and a few mothers, too—navigate the murky bureaucracy around child support and parenting.

This is how the faith-based non-profit, Divine Alternatives for DADS Services, or DADS, came into being—built around the belief that fathers are the cornerstone of a healthy family. Fatherlessness in this country, they say, is at the root of $100 billion in annual costs to the federal government. "It's the true breakdown of the family," Jeanett said. "Generation on top of generation—grandmothers, and aunties raising kids without a father present."

From its offices along Rainier Avenue, DADS provides services around child support and parenting and offers counseling and education aimed at empowering men to become more responsible and accountable fathers. "There's not a man in this country who doesn't want to be his children's hero," Marvin told a Congressional subcommittee when he was invited to speak in Washington.

Back in 2001, the couple had worked alongside Haynes as he tried to get the state to modify his child support payments to fit his budget. He even eventually got the $133,000 he owed whittled down to a more manageable $11,000.

On top of that, Haynes, now 49 and married, created a parenting plan that allowed him to be a father to his children, including a reunion with his twins, a boy and girl, who had been adopted and taken out of state while he was in prison. Two of his kids are now in college, another is in the U.S. Marine Corps Forces Reserve, and the other two are raising families of their own.

"Marvin and Jeanett take a holistic approach, helping you confront the issues that caused you to be in trouble or away from your kids in the first place," said Haynes. "They make it so a person can stand on their feet and be supportive of themselves and their kids," he continued. "They don't just talk about it, they model it as well."

State: *Most men can relate to some part of the struggle that Bill experienced. The following questions will help examine some of those shared struggles.*

[Read the questions and allow for time to discuss the question.]

Process Questions

1. How do drugs interfere with being a father?
2. What impact does incarceration have on being a father?
3. How can you be a dad if you can't get a job?
4. What is the mission of the child support system?
5. What are all the things that children need from their father?
6. What kind of help do dads need?

[Summarize the answers.]

State: *This curriculum is about making a commitment to be the dad your child needs, to make and live up to the statement that, "I will daddy up!"*

Summarize: *Facing the truth about our situation may hurt, but we can only heal. If we never face the truth, then one day the truth will face us. Remember, a lie always kills.*

Transition: *Next, we will take a closer look at your life.*

1.3 It can be hard for a man to be a dad but even harder for a child to be without one.

1.4 This Is Your Life

> rct 315 | rst 15 | est 5 | page 16
>
> **State:** *Just like Bill has a story, so do you. What were the good and bad experiences that helped shape your life?*
>
> **Instruct:** *Reflect over your life and select three good and bad experiences that may have shaped you. Describe the event, what you thought or felt through it, and how it might have shaped or influenced your life.*

Just like William had a story, so do you. When you think back over your life, you can soon realize that certain events or experiences help shape who you are. This shaping is done by the good things that happen in your life, as well as the bad. What were the bad things that happened in William's life? What were the good things that happened in William's life? In this next exercise, everyone will have an opportunity to look at their life and identify the good and bad things they've experienced.

Instructions: Reflect over your life and select three good and bad experiences that may have shaped you. Describe the event, what you thought or felt through it, and how it might have shaped or influenced your life.

Good Experiences

	Event	Thought or Feeling	Action
1			
2			
3			

Bad Experiences

	Event	Thought or Feeling	Action
1			
2			
3			

> **State:** *Because these questions are personal, you do not have to share anything you don't want to. Also, let's all be respectful towards those who are willing to share.*
>
> [Read the process questions.]

Process questions:

1. Would you like to share any good experiences?
2. Would you like to share any bad experiences?
3. When you have a good or bad experience, how can you make a choice to move backward, stay there, or move forward?

> **State:** *When dads face tough experiences, they have a choice to move backward, stay there, or move forward.*
>
> **Transition:** *Next, we will examine what it takes to make an actual change.*

1.5 When dads face tough experiences, they have a choice to move backward, stay there, or move forward.

1.6 Change

> rct 310 | rst 10 | est 5 | page 18
>
> **State:** *Change may be simple, but it is rarely easy. In this section, we will explore the motivation for change, what you need to change, and how to make a change.*
>
> **State:** *Next, we will look at what needs to change.*
>
> **Note:** Pay attention to how participants respond when you read the instructions to the second part. Often participants will exhibit facial expressions, gestures, or sounds of resisting the exercise. You might remind them of what you observe (hear and see).
>
> [Read the instructions.]

Instructions: Sign your name in the first box below. When done, please wait for the instructions from the facilitator before proceeding.

Instructions: Next sign your name in the second box using your other hand.

> [Read the process questions.]

Process Questions

1. How did you feel when you were asked to sign your name in the box another way?
2. Did it come naturally, or did you have to stop and think about it?
3. Were you comfortable with doing this differently from your normal process?
4. What are some things that would make us resistant to change?

Change is not comfortable.

> [Read the process questions.]
>
> [Below are some sample responses you can share in case they are not shared by participants.]
> Habit—*I am so used to doing it a certain way.*
> Time—*I've done it this way for a long time.*
> Effort—*It is not easy to change.*
> Failure—*Every time I change, I change back.*
>
> **Ask:** *Would someone volunteer to read about "homeostasis"?*

The concept of homeostasis is from the field of biology. The human body regulates itself to keep a steady-state, or homeostasis (Cannon, 1932). An example is when blood sugar is too high, the body thirsts for water in an attempt to dilute the sugar levels to return it back to equilibrium. In short, any change in the body is met with resistance and an attempt to change it back.

This concept is also used in family therapy, related to the idea that families and individuals resist change in order to maintain a steady state. This is what keeps families and individuals locked in certain cycles or behaviors, even if those cycles are destructive—it's like a car getting stuck in a rut. The car wheel is trying to roll forward, but cannot get the momentum to break free and rolls right back into the rut.

Seligman and Maier (1967) conducted classical condition research, in which dogs associated a shock with another stimulus and exhibited learned helplessness. A similar experiment was repeated for humans using loud sounds that resulted in similar outcomes. We must consider the experiences that people go through and learn how it shapes them and their responses. Some people have learned to be helpless and it is not easy to change this learned behavior.

Process Questions

1. What do you think about the statement, "Change is not always natural or easy, but it is often necessary."?
2. What are some examples of changes you have tried to make, but have found it difficult?

Change is not easy. When we try to change, we often change back to our old patterns.

The Stages of Change Model is widely used in the field of addiction counseling as a way to understand how people are motivated to change. There are five stages that people cycle through several times before they actually make a change (Prochaska, DiClemente and Norcross, 1992).

Stages of Change Model
Prochaska, 1992

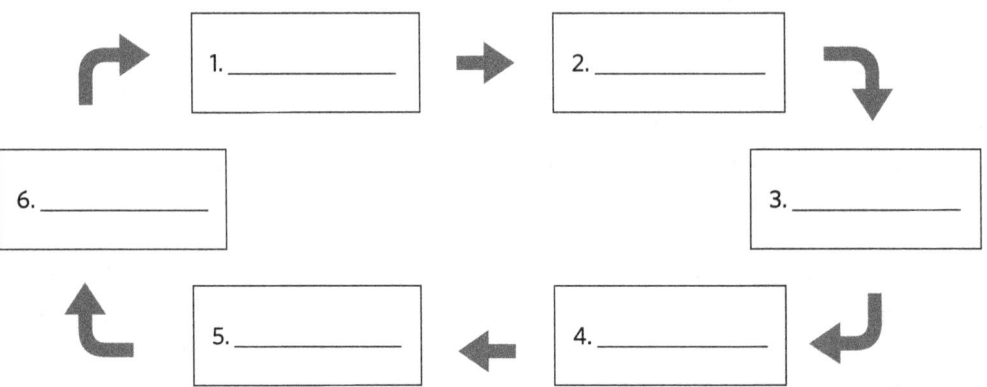

Instructions: Fill in the stages in the diagram using the following definitions to match following words: (Maintenance, Preparation, Relapse, Pre-contemplation, Action, Contemplation).

1. The dad does not see a need to change right now.
2. The dad sees a need for change and is thinking about changing.
3. The dad intends to take action in the near future.

4. The dad makes changes in behavior.
5. The dad needs to sustain the change and not slip back into the rut.
6. The dad starts again with the change.

1.6 The success or failure (feedback) of a person making a change is based on a series of stages and the strength of the motivation of the change.

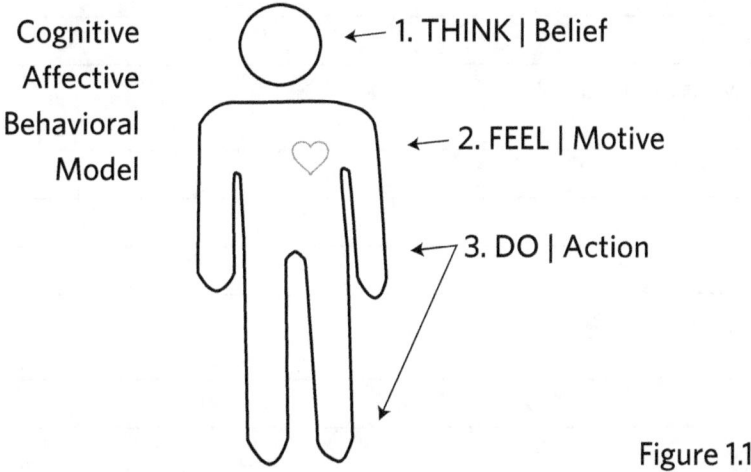

Figure 1.1

One visual aid of making a change is turning our life around. It is making a 180-degree turn. This idea is summarized in the concept of repentance. It is turning from one way and turning to another way. How do we begin to make a change?

The Better Dad model can help guide our change. The model is about aligning what you think, feel, and do to become a better dad for your child. In this section, we will write out a core belief, a passion, and an action that will help guide and motivate us to be a better dad. The following is an example of this model:

Example:

1. My main belief (think) is that a father is responsible for his child.
2. My motivation (feel) is that my child's life is more important than my own.
3. My change (do) is to help my child grow and develop.

Instructions: Write down your main belief, motivation, and change that will help make you a better dad.

1. What is your main belief?

   _____
   _____
   _____
   _____

2. What is your motivation?

   _____
   _____
   _____
   _____

3. What is your change?

   _____
   _____
   _____
   _____

State: *Let's take a few minutes to share our change with one other person.*

Ask: *Pair up with someone seated next to you and share with one another what you have written down.*

Note: *If there is an odd number, have one group of three.*

State: *Your change can also be used for your Dad Plan.*

1.7 The Dad Plan

> rct 305 | rst 5 | est 5 | page 23
>
> **State:** *This section is one of the most important parts of the course, where you put knowledge into action.*
>
> **Instruct:** *Answer the following questions to create your Dad Plan, in order to become a better dad by turning your life around.*

Fathering Skill: Become a better dad by turning my life around

Instructions: Answer the following questions to create your Dad Plan to become a better dad.

1. What is my specific SMART (Specific, Measurable, Achievable, Realistic, Timetable) goal for turning my life around?
2. What can I do every day this week to grow more culturally aware?
3. When and where will I do this?
4. Who will hold me accountable?

2.0 Every Dad's Challenge: Being There

> rct 300 | rst 60 | est 15 | page 24
>
> [Read the following]

GOAL

To become a better dad,
I will commit to being there,
for the sake of my child,
by investing this time here.

OBJECTIVES

1. Fatherlessness
2. Fatherfulness
3. A lifetime commitment as a father, not a life sentence without one

Commitment is a verb. It is an action word. Commitment is a pledge to do something. Helping our child develop in every way requires the commitment of being there. Fathering is rewarding, but also requires some hard work. And without commitment, hard work does not get done.

We need to resolve to be the father who is there for his children. To overcome any barriers to fathering, a man must have a strong commitment. How strong is your commitment to your children? You may say you are willing to die for your children, but are you willing to daily live for them no matter what you face? Our commitment should be in words and deeds.

2.1 FatherLESSness

> **Ask:** *Have you ever heard the term "fatherlessness"? What does it mean to be fatherless and what is the impact?*
>
> **State:** *In this section, we will examine fatherlessness and its impact.*

2.1. Want Ad for a Dad

> **State:** *In the next fun activity you have a chance to be a child again. We can potentially learn from this activity.*
>
> *[Read the following instructions.]*

Instructions: Imagine being an eight-year-old child again and you don't have a father. What would you want in a father? Take two minutes to write a want ad for the type of dad you would want from a child's perspective. Include the duties, salary, and benefits of being a father (Williams, 2010).

> **State:** *I would like to give you a chance to share your ad.*
>
> **Ask:** *Who would like to share?*
>
> **Note:** Make sure you give encouragement for those who do share. When asking the process questions, you can use questions number three and four as questions they just think about rather than answer aloud.
>
> [Read the following instructions.]

Process Questions:

1. Why did you write what you wrote?
2. What does your ad say about you?
3. Could you answer your own ad?
4. What do you think your child would write?

> **Note:** This exercise uncovers our own personal definition of the role of a father. Question three explores whether or not we live up to our own definition. Question four explores what our child definition might be. Often, children don't know how to express what they need from their dads.
>
> **Transition:** *This exercise uncovers our own personal definition of the role of the father. Next, we will look at the definition and impact of fatherlessness.*
>
> [Read or summarize the following section.]

2.1.b Defining Fatherlessness

Traditionally, when we hear about absent fathers, we relate it to fathers that are physically absent. However, a father can be absent in other ways, such as socially, emotionally, morally, and/or spiritually. A father can live in the home (physically present), but he may also be absent socially and emotionally.

Father absence can be a permanent or temporary state in which systemic or personal barriers and/or choices prevent a father from providing his resources or social capital to his child. Examples of systemic barriers that make it difficult or impossible for the father to be involved in his child's life may include incarceration (wrongful), war, severe mental or physical disability, a hostile divorce or separation, or death.

Fathers can also make personal choices that prevent their involvement. Some choices that lead to personal barriers of involvement include addiction, lack of physical and mental health maintenance, risky behaviors, irresponsibility, abandonment, crime, career choices, child abuse and neglect, and incarceration. It is possible the reason for the absence may lessen aspects of the impact on the child. However, the results are the same no matter the circumstances and that is the forfeiture of the provision of social capital for the child.

> **Note:** The following illustration shows how a father provides resources that funnel into his child's life. Review this diagram and share what the resources or capital for his child.
>
> **State:** *Let's review this diagram of resources that a father provides for his child.*
>
> [Review the diagram.]

EVERY DAD'S CHALLENGE: BEING THERE 27

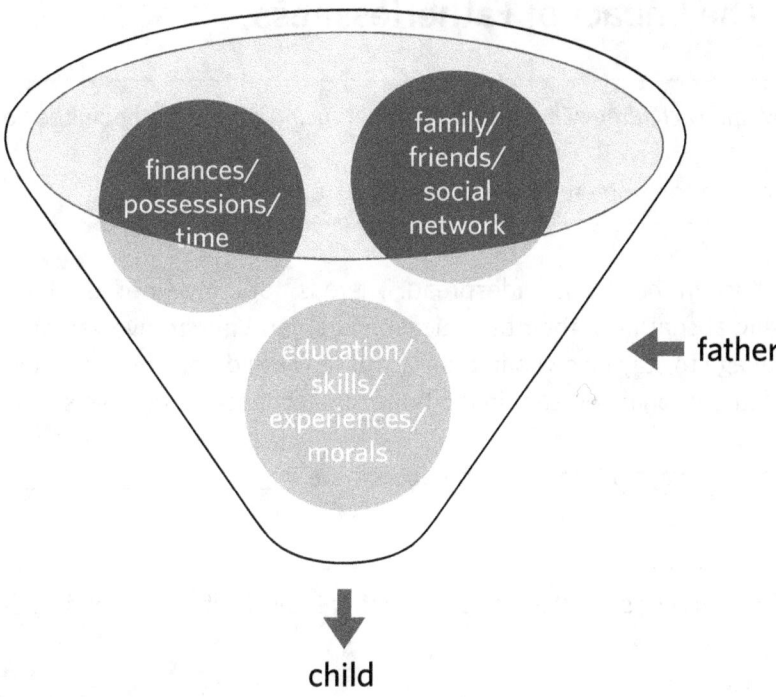

(Williams, 2010)

A father absence is when a father—through barriers or personal choice—abandons providing the resources or support physically, mentally, socially, emotionally, financially, and/or spiritually for his child.

Process Questions:

1. What are some of the other things a father provides for his child?
2. What is an example of physical, mental, social, emotional, financial and spiritual absence?

> **Transition:** *Next, let's look at the impact of fatherlessness.*
>
> [Review the diagram.]

2.1.c The Impact of Fatherlessness

> **Ask:** *How many children will go to bed without their biological father in the home?*
>
> [Read or have someone read the following paragraph.]

Father absence in the U.S. is widespread. There is not a one-to-one relationship between fathers living absent from their biological children and father involvement. Many of these fathers manage to stay involved in the lives of their children. However, the opposite is also true, that fathers can be present in the home and absent in other ways.

1. The four ways a father can be absent are P_____, E_____, S_____ and M_____.

> **Share:** *The four ways a father can be absent are* Physically, Emotionally, Spiritually, *and* Morally.
>
> [Read or have someone read the following paragraph.]

Princeton sociologist, Sara McLanahan, a single mother, set out to prove that single motherhood did not negatively impact the well-being of children. The more she investigated the more evidence she found that supported the opposite conclusion (McLanahan & Sandefur, 1994).

2. Children in single mother families fared p_____ across a wide range of outcomes including: financial, emotional, behavioral, legal and sexual.

> **Share:** *Children in single mother families fare poorly across a wide range of outcomes including: financial, emotional, behavioral, legal and sexual.*
>
> [Read or have someone read the following paragraph.]

Childhood poverty in America is affected by a father's absence in the family. Less than a third of children living in two-parent homes lived below the poverty level, while 70% of children living in single-mother families lived below the poverty level in 2009 (Mather, 2010). Poverty can be viewed as an accelerator to many other outcomes because of the inherent lack of support and resources of this condition. Also, there is a chance for a repeating generational cycle.

> **State:** *So, what does the research say about the impact of father absence. There are literally hundreds of research articles that report the impact of father absence. Let's review a few key articles.*
>
> [Read or summarize the following research articles.]

Following is a list of other research findings of the negative impact of father absence on the outcome of children:

- When fathers are absent, their children are at higher risk of suffering from negative outcomes, including emotional and behavioral problems, poverty, child abuse and neglect, substance abuse, low educational attainment, and teen pregnancy (McLanahan & Sandefur, 1994; Angel & Angel, 1996; Mott, Kowaleski-Jones, & Menaghen, 1997; Hoffmann & Johnson, 1998; Brown, Cohen, Johnson, & Salzinger, 1998).
- Data from the National Longitudinal Survey of Youth indicated that a father's absence significantly increased by two times the likelihood of difficulties with peers, depressive behavior in boys, and other behavioral challenges for girls (Mott, 1993).
- A population-based survey study that included one million children revealed that children from single-parent homes were at twice the risk of mental disorders, suicide and attempted suicide, and alcohol or drug abuse compared to two-parent families (Weitoft, Hjern, Haglund, & Rosen, 2003).
- Students living in father-absent homes were twice as likely to repeat a grade and 1.7 times more likely to drop out of high school than children living with both parents (McNeal, 1995; Nord & West, 2001).
- Research on non-intact families found that the lower the quantity and quality of biological father involvement during childhood, the lower the level of adult child education, employment, income, physical health, social attainment, sobriety, sexual fidelity, parental success, paternal closeness, and happiness (Williams, 2016).

> **State:** *After reviewing these research articles, it is not a stretch to make the following statement.*
>
> **Share:** *Willful father absence is a form of* Child Abuse *and* Neglect.
>
> [Read or have someone read the following paragraph.]

2. Willful father absence is a form of C_____ A_____ and N_____ (Williams, 2010).

2.1 The result of father absence places his child at a higher risk for many negative outcomes.

> [Ask the following process questions. Be sure to encourage those who share by repeating what they say, thanking them for their comments, asking them to say or expanding on their comments.]

Process Questions:

1. What do you think about fathers who are absent?
2. What is the impact on the children?
3. Have you been absent in the life of your child?

2.2 FatherFULLness

> rct 285 | rst 45 | est 15 | page 28
>
> **Transition:** *In this section, we will look at the concept of fatherfullness. To start, we will examine what children say about fatherfullness by reviewing an example of a child's essay.*
>
> [Summarize, read or ask someone to share the following.]

2.2.a What Children Say About FatherFULLness

Since 1992, the National Center for Fathering has collected over 1,000,000 essays written by kindergarten through twelfth grade students describing what their father or father-figure means to them. One interesting finding in these essays is that even in the cases where children have written about absent or "bad" fathers, they would still share they needed them. The children would describe the hurt caused by their father's absence or poor fathering, but finish with something like, "I still want him to know I love him and need him." The following is an example of a typical positive essay, written by a first grader.

> [Make sure they know this was written by a first grader. Read it to the group. Afterwards share the process questions.]

My father is the best.
My dad helps me when I'm hurt.
He plays with me a lot.
He makes breakfast for my family.
He lets me have friends over.
My dad helps me ride my bike.
When he gets home, we turn on a movie and cuddle. We cuddle with each other a lot.
He plays soccer with me.
He helps me do my math.
He helps me read.
My dad was the second person who held me when I was just born.
My dad is in the Air Force and he saves our country.
My dad is a very good dad.
Thank you, Dad, for being my hero and my dad.
I love you.
(National Center for Fathering, 2015)

Process Questions:

1. Is there anything in this child's essay that stands out to you?
2. Why would children still have a place in their heart for absent dads?

2.2.b How Research Defines FatherFULLness

> **Transition:** *Next, we'll look at what research defines fatherfullness.*
>
> [Summarize, read or ask someone to share the following.]

Examining further the importance of the role of the father requires exploring what fathers do, why and when they do it, and how might it make a difference for children. One of the most researched concepts when it comes to the roles of fathers is involvement (Williams, 2016).

Outside the realm of biology, fatherhood is a social construct that defines a father's involvement with his child. The construct of fatherhood has transitioned over time throughout American history from a role with the main emphasis on a father's participation as a moral teacher, a household provider, and a nurturing father (Williams). These one-dimensional constructs of fatherhood are descriptive of the ways fathers, during historical time periods, were expected to be involved with their children (Williams).

The concept of father involvement has evolved to explain the many diverse ways fathers, in different circumstances and situations, interact to positively influence the outcomes of their children. Accessibility, involvement, and responsibility are three basic components that have become universal to most definitions of father involvement (Williams). These components can be framed as society's perception of what children need from fathers (responsibility), how available the fathers are to meet their children's needs (accessibility), and how responsive fathers are to the needs of their children (engagement).

> [Give participants a chance to provide the correct word for the blank.]
>
> **Share:** *A father provides essential* AIR *for his children.*
> **Share:** *A father is* Accessible *by being there or available to be reached by his child.*
> **Share:** *A father is* Involved *by being engaged in every part of his child's life.*
> **Share:** *A father is* Responsive *to meet the needs of his child.*

A father provides essential **AIR** for his children.

1. A father is A_____ by being there or available to be reached by his child.
2. A father is I_____ by being engaged in every part of his child's life.
3. A father is R_____ to meet the needs of his child.
(Williams, 2010)

> [Read or invite someone to read the summary statement. Ask if anyone has any questions or comments.]

2.2 A father provides AIR (Accessibility, Involvement & Responsibility) to help meet the physical, social, emotional and spiritual needs of children.

2.2.c What Research Says about FatherFULLness

> **Transition:** *Next, we'll look at what research defines fatherfullness.*
>
> [Summarize, read or ask someone to share the following]

Here are some of the studies that confirm Rohner and Veneziano's findings documenting the positive benefits fathers bring to their children socially, behaviorally, and academically:

- A study on empathy in adulthood found that the strongest predictor of empathy for others (men and women) was the level of care and support by fathers in childhood (Koestner & Weinberger, 1990).
- Another series of investigations reported higher levels of self-control and fewer behavioral problems in school children with involved fathers (Amato & Rivera, 1999). In addition, these children were found to have higher levels of social skills, self-esteem and general life skills (Amato & Rivera).
- Data from the National Study of Families and Households showed that, when fathers were positively involved, children experienced fewer behavior problems and anxieties, got along better with others, and were more responsible (Mosely & Thomson, 1995).
- Summarizing an early study on a father's influence on young children, researchers indicated that a father's interest and involvement in the early years was strongly

associated with higher cognitive functioning and greater academic achievement among school-age children (Biller & Kimpton, 1997).
- A Department of Education study found that children whose fathers were highly involved in their schools were more likely to do well academically, enjoy school, participate in extracurricular activities and were less likely to repeat a grade or be expelled out of school than children whose fathers were not involved (Nord & West, 2001).
- Studies on non-intact families found that the higher the quantity and quality of biological father involvement during childhood, the higher the level of adult child education, employment, income, physical health, social attainment, sobriety, sexual fidelity, parental success, paternal closeness, and happiness (Williams, 2016).

State: *After reviewing these research articles, it is not a stretch to make the following statement.*

Share: *Willful father absence is a form of* Child Abuse *and* Neglect.

[Read or have someone read the following paragraph.]

2.3 A Lifetime Commitment as a Father

rct 285 | rst 30 | est 15 | page 31

State: *Another part of fatherFULLness is commitment.*

Instruct: *I will read the following story and would like for you to keep in mind the topic of this lesson of committed nurturing. I will ask you a few questions to process the story afterward. Right now, sit back and use your imagination as you travel through the world of Amos in "The Amos Story."*

Note: *This is a powerful story—as you read, ensure that it "comes alive" for listeners.*

2.3.a The Amos Story

The Amos Story

Amos left the hot cotton fields with rocks in his stomach. Earlier in the day, Clete, a house slave, had overheard a conversation between the plantation master and another man about how much money Amos should bring at the auction the next day, and he immediately told Amos.

Amos was a hard-working slave. He never complained about the long, hard, hot hours in the sun. He always met his daily quota for picking cotton, and he often helped the other slaves with their quota as well. By most plantation master's standards, Amos was an ideal slave. He should bring a nice bundle to the slave master.

Amos and Beulah had seven children. Being sold—and the resulting splitting up of the family—was always a grim possibility. But the sudden reality for Amos and Beulah was horrifying. They made great effort not to show the children their fear and anguish as they had supper and prepared the one room shanty for the night's rest.

Amos and his three sons unfolded the hand-made blankets and placed them as pallets in their usual places on the dirt floor. Beulah brushed and plaited the hair of the four little girls. When they were ready for bed, Amos gathered the family around him and quoted by memory, because he could not read, the first verse of Psalm 23, "De Lord is my shepherd. I shall not want." Then he prayed for the family and for their rest. He even prayed for the slave master and his family. His prayer was short tonight. He wanted to stay in control of his emotions. Yet, in his heart he was in great turmoil.

Beulah blew out the candle at the end of the small room where the children lay waiting to fall off to sleep. The children did not suspect the horrifying situation facing their mother and father. Almost in unison, they said, "Ga-nite, Momma. Ga-nite, Daddy."

In the dimly lit part of the other half of the room, near the only door, Amos held Beulah tight. He kissed her on the forehead and whispered in her ear, "I'm goin' out fer while." Knowing Amos like she did, Beulah felt he probably wanted to go pray. "Git cha some rest," he whispered as he opened the door to go out.

Amos found a spot he had used many times, back in the far corner of the big barn. There was a pile of hay there. He fell immediately on the pile and wept bitterly. He had held back his emotions since early morning when Clete had told him about the master's plan. He had cut his prayer time short with his family cause this flood was just behind the dam. His heart was broken. The pain was unbearable. Beulah and the seven children were his life. It was his dream that if he worked hard and pleased the master that his children might earn special privileges and be pulled from the harsh conditions of the cotton fields to learn trades on the plantation, and especially learn to read. Many nights in this very spot, he had prayed that they would all stay together as a family. Now his dream was about to be shattered. It was as if a jagged-edged knife was being ripped through his heart.

After what seemed like hours of sobbing, Amos sat up and began to think about his options. Clete had urged him to run away in the night. Amos had considered that option much of the day, but he could not assure himself that this was the safest option for a runaway slave. And should he remain alive and make it to the North, he was not comforted that he and his family could be reunited someday.

As the seconds and minutes crept closer to the dreaded dawn, Amos thrashed around on the dirt ground and the pile of hay. No doubt the animals in the barn spent a sleepless night as well. They couldn't see Amos, but they could certainly hear him plead with God for help.

Soon, the early light of day began to peer through the cracks in the old barn. The roosters crowed. Amos knew his fate was before him. In a stupor, he gathered himself up. He opened the door of the barn and walked behind the barn to the lumber pile. He sat on a large tree stump. He placed his left arm on a nearby anvil. He raised his right arm high in the air. Without a single moment's hesitation, he slammed the hatchet he was holding down on his left arm. A deep, raw scream ripped out of his belly that could be heard throughout the slave quarters. In the woodpile, at his feet, lay a bloody hatchet and his left hand and wrist: the cost of a daddy to keep a slave family together.

Within minutes of that bloodcurdling scream, several of the slave men rushed to the back of the barn. Beulah sat up from her near sleepless night on her pallet. She knew that scream belonged to Amos. She told their oldest son to help the children get dressed while she went to the barn. She ran out the door and met other slaves running behind the barn. There she pushed her way through the emotional crowd to see Amos holding his severed left arm. There was blood everywhere. Beulah gasped at the sight. But the horror of the scene quickly turned to bitter/sweet emotions for her, because she knew immediately that Amos would no longer be considered for the slave auction later that day. No master would want a mutilated slave "boy."

(Genovese, 1976).

Process Questions:

1. What stood out to you in this story?
2. What can we learn from Amos?
3. How can you apply this to your own life?

> **State:** *This is the embellished account of how one slave father committed himself to his role as father and husband. Here was a man, a slave man, who cared so much for his family that he would sever his left arm.*
>
> **State:** *Amos did not run from his challenges to be committed. He did not abandon his family. He did not run to his fellow slave brothers to sit around and complain about his condition. He did not drown himself in alcohol or drugs to eliminate or subdue his hurt and pain.*
>
> **State:** *Amos was committed to his family and he had the courage to face the horrific challenge before him. His heart beat big and strong for his family. Where does this commitment begin for us?*

2.3.b What Being Your Child's Father Means to You

> **Ask:** *Have you ever received a personal letter in the mail from someone important to you? Wasn't that a special experience? What would it mean to your child if you wrote them a personal letter or drew or colored them a picture of your commitment?*
>
> **State:** *Verbalizing our commitment to our child(ren) is reassuring for them and provides a sense of belonging. It's like choosing them to be on your team. Putting it in writing allows our child to treasure the experience.*
>
> [Read or have someone read the following paragraph.]

Commitment Letter

Instructions: Write a letter to your child or draw a picture that expresses your commitment. The letter is suggested to be 300 words or less (that would be about one page or three paragraphs). You can have the letter mailed to your child to make the experience more memorable.

2.4 The Dad Plan

> rct 255 | rst 15 | est 15 | page 35
>
> **State:** *This section is one of the most important parts of the course, where you put knowledge into action.*
>
> **Instruct:** *Answer the following questions to create your Dad Plan to become a better dad that commits to being there.*

Fathering Skill: To become a better dad, I commit to being there.

Instructions: Answer the following questions to create your Dad Plan to become a better dad.

1. What is my specific SMART (Specific, Measurable, Achievable, Realistic, Timetable) goal for growing in cultural awareness?

2. What can I do every day this week to grow more culturally aware?

3. When and where will I do this?

4. Who will hold me accountable?

3.0 What Men Do

> rct 240 | rst 60 | est 15 | page 36
>
> [Read the following.]

GOAL

To become a better dad,
I will do what men do:
mature, respect women, and love and serve others.
And that includes my children too.

OBJECTIVES

1. Man Up
2. Marry Up
3. Daddy Up

When did you become a man? As I have asked men this question through the years, I have noticed a perplexing look on many faces. For these men who have ranged from 15 to 55, no one has ever asked them this question, so they have not given it much thought. The answers vary from taking responsibility for one's self to procreation. Noticeably absent are matters of character.

Manhood is an assisted journey of maturity and service in respect, responsibility, and righteousness in all his relationships. When a man learns his role, he is positioned to achieve his mission for life, because this man knows who he is and what his purpose is in life. We don't have to have "arrived" to be a dad but we must be on the journey. Walking through the door of manhood, we leave behind our boyish ways. We cannot lead our sons in a journey we have never begun, and that is why it takes a man to be a dad!

3.1 Man Up

> **Note:** This activity introduces the characteristics of being a man. Please remember generalizing is good for research and humor, but it does not apply for many other cases.
>
> [Read the instructions below.]

Instructions: Most people recognize the symbol for a man. While that may not be hard, the real challenge is determining what are the two objects that make up the symbol for men.

Note: Give the class a chance to try to figure this out. You may consider giving a small prize for the person who can guess the answer.

[After they have tried to answer you can give the following clue.]

State: *Here is a clue. Men are from Mars.*

[After giving them a chance, you can give the following answer.]

Answer: *Mars was the Greek god of war. The two objects in the symbol for a man are a shield and spear.*

Summarize: *Men share many similarities with women but there are also differences that can be a source of conflict. For example, men are generalized to be more rational and about winning or performance. Let's take a closer look at some considerations about men.*

3.1.a Activity: What Kind of Man are You?

Note: This small group activity requires space to gather the men in a circle. You have the option of using chairs or an 8.5 x 11" paper on the floor.

State: *This is a physical activity and if you have any mobility trouble, you are free not to move from your spot.*

State: *Take your place in the circle on the paper or in the chair. On a count of three, we will ask the person in the middle, "What kind of person are you?" They will reply with any characteristic of a man (e.g., I am a man who loves his family). If that characteristic does not apply to you, stay put; otherwise, you must move from the chair or paper to a different one. The last person in the middle who does not have a chair or paper is the next person to be asked, "What type of man are you?"*

[Give them a one-minute warning when the time is up.]

Instructions: Take your place in the circle on the paper or in the chair. On a count of three we will ask the person in the middle, "What kind of person are you?" They will reply with any characteristic of a man (e.g., I am a man who loves his family). If that characteristic does not apply to you, stay put; otherwise, you must move from the chair or paper to a different one. The last person in the middle who does not have a chair or paper is the next person to be asked, "What type of man are you?"

> **State:** *This exercise gave us a picture of some of characteristics of being a man. Next, let's explore some questions that take us a little deeper about what it means to be a man.*

Process Questions :

1. When did you become a man?
2. What are the ingredients for being a man?
3. Who prepares you to be a man?
4. Can a woman teach a boy to be a man?

> **Note:** For question 1 ask everyone to give you an age with no explanation. The answer to question 1 is dependent on how you define being a man.
> [Ask question 1.]
>
> **State:** *Unfortunately, in the U.S. there is no universal definition of what it means to be a man.*
>
> [Ask question 2.]
>
> **State:** *These ingredients you shared are a part of what it means to be a man.*
>
> [Ask question 3.]
>
> **State:** *The expectation is that a father would help prepare a boy to become a man.*
>
> **Note:** For question 4, ask everyone to raise their hand if they believe a woman can teach a boy how to be a man. The answer to question 4 is based on how you interpret the question.
>
> [Ask question 4.]
>
> **State:** *In my opinion, a woman can teach a boy how to be a man, but not bring him into manhood. You cannot bring someone into something you have not arrived in.*
>
> **Transition:** *Next, we'll look at a story that gives us some insight to another aspect of manhood.*

3.1.b The Elephant in the Room

Show the Delinquent Elephants Video

> **Note:** This activity involves a video. In the case where you do not have access to the video, do not have time, or do not have the ability to show the video, you can read the account of the story below.
>
> **State:** *In late 1990's, in South Africa's Pilanesberg Park, rhinos were thriving until an unknown killer began stalking them. Thirty-nine rhinos, 10 percent of the population in the park, were killed. It turned out that young male elephants were behind the murders of rhinos.*
>
> **State:** *The problem went back 20 years to South Africa's largest conservation area, Kruger National Park. Kruger had too many elephants. In those days, there was no way to relocate these large adults. So, researchers decided to kill the adults and save the children, who were more easily transported to other parks.*
>
> **State:** *Years later, those lonely orphans developed into a gang of troubled teenagers. That's when the killings at Pilanesberg Park began. The people at Pilanesberg wanted to avoid killing the delinquents. The rangers began looking for role models to keep the youngsters from mating at an early age when they couldn't handle increased testosterone levels. They decided to bring in some even larger bull elephants.*
>
> **State:** *The rangers at Kruger National Park brought in some of these big elephants. The bigger, older elephants established a new hierarchy, in part by sparring with the younger elephants to discourage them from being sexually active. That means less testosterone, and that was good news for the rhinos.*
>
> [Ask the process questions.]

Process Questions :

1. What stands out to you about this video?
2. How can you compare this video to the pathway for boys to become men?
3. What do immature males do?
4. What is the main goal of being a man?
5. What is standing in the way of male maturing?

> **State:** *Comparatively, this story highlights the need that boys have for their fathers to assist them on their journey to manhood. In the story, the group of teenagers lost their way without having their fathers serve a function to confront them or keep them in check on the right pathway to maturity. The fathers were role models and teachers.*

3.1.c What Do Men Do?

> **Note:** Background information on being a man.
>
> [Read the instructions.]

Instructions: Solve the crossword puzzle. Use the words to fill in the blanks to complete the definition of manhood.

Down
1. Showing value and worth for others
3. Owning your words and actions
5. A pathway to a goal destination
7. Someone helps you

Across
2. Our social connections to others
4. Doing the right thing at the right time
6. A state of growth and development
8. When you help others

Manhood is an 7. _____ 5. _____ of 6. _____ and 8. _____ in 1. _____, 3. _____ and 4. _____ in all his 2. _____.

> **State:** *Next, we are going to discuss the process questions about the definition of manhood and read some points about the definition to consider.*

Process Questions:

1. Can we become a man on our own?
2. What is the journey of manhood?
3. What does a mature man look like?
4. How can we be a man for others?
5. To whom should respect be given?
6. What does it mean to be responsible?
7. Why is righteousness important in a man's life?
8. What are the different types of a man's relationships?

Assisted: We need assistance or help to become men and it should start with our fathers and continues with our sons (and daughters for womanhood).

Journey: Manhood is more of a journey or process rather than a destination.

Maturity: You were a child and now as a man you put childish things behind you.

Service: When we were babies, others served us; when were boys, we served ourselves. As men, we now serve others.

Respect: All my relationships start with respect or valuing myself and others in what I think, feel, say, and do.

Responsibility: Being responsible is taking ownership for what we do and say and for possessions.

Righteousness: "Righteousness" is doing the right thing, at the right time, for the right reasons.

Relationship: Part of our main purpose is to socially connect to others, which holds the key to our life, growth, and future.

Instructions: From this section, describe one thing you would like to improve on in your journey of manhood.

_____

_____

_____

_____

3.2 Marry Up

rct 225 | rst 45 | est 15 | page 50

Note: This activity introduces the perceived differences of women. Please remember generalizing is good for research and humor but it does not apply for many other cases.

[Read the instructions below.]

Instructions: Most people recognize the symbol represents women. While that may not be hard, the real challenge is determining what are the two objects that make up the symbol for a woman.

> **Note:** Give the class a chance to try to figure this out. You may consider giving a small prize for the person who can guess the answer.
>
> [After they have tried to answer you can give the following clue.]
>
> **State:** *Here is a clue. Women are from Venus.*
>
> [After giving them a chance you can give the following answer.]
>
> **Answer:** *Venus is the Greek goddess of love or beauty. The two objects in the symbol for a woman are a mirror and a comb.*
>
> **Summarize:** *Women share many similarities with men but there are also differences that can be a source of conflict. For example, women are generalized to be more emotional and about relationships. Let's take a closer look at some considerations about women.*

3.2a Your History with Women

> **Note:** For this activity, you will need a marker board or flip chart and markers.
>
> This activity attempts to get men to list all the qualities they would want in a wife. The men are likely to have many ideal qualities to list. The purpose is using this list to shock them with the question of how many of these ideal qualities are true of *them* personally. Are they a good *man*?
>
> This activity is divided into two parts. In the first part, you give the men the time to write down their top five qualities of a good woman. In the second part, you compile a comprehensive of their top qualities of a good woman.
>
> **Instruct:** *Next we will do an activity called "a good woman is hard to find." Take a minute to write a list of your top 5 qualities of a good woman. Once you complete the list, I will guide you through the second part.*

A Good Woman Is Hard to Find

Instructions: Take a minute to write a list of your top five qualities of a good woman.

1. _____
2. _____
3. _____
4. _____
5. _____

> **Instruct:** *Next we are going to compile a comprehensive list of the qualities of a good woman. Let's take turns sharing the qualities and give me time to write them down.*

Process Questions:

1. How many of these qualities are true of you?
2. Do you have to be a good man to find a good woman?
3. What can we learn from this exercise?

> **Summarize:** *One thing we can take away from this exercise is the importance of working on ourselves. We tend to attract people who may not necessarily be the same as us, but compatible to us. In other words, one type of bad gets attracted to another type of bad. And when one person grows or matures a type of good, then what attracted us can become what repels us from someone.*

Relationship Foundation with Women

> **Instruct:** *Fill in the blank.*
>
> [Your mother can SHAPE how you relate to women.]

Instruct: Fill in the blank.

Your mother can s_____ how you relate to women.

> **State:** *Many men do not care to read, but the following information has been helpful to many men. So, next we will take time to read and learn about our relationship with women based on our attachment to our mother.*
>
> [You can give the men an opportunity to read, but you should start and try to make the reading come alive. Also invite them to underline or mark anything that stands out to you.]

Attachment to Your Mom

The ability for people to trust is rooted in the early relationship with their mother as a primary caregiver. This attachment is a deep and enduring emotional bond that connects one person to another. The theory on attachment provides an explanation of how the parent-child relationship emerges and influences subsequent development and future relationships (Bowlby, 1969).

If, during the first three months of their lives, their mothers were responsive to the child's needs, then the child became securely attached and more trusting in future adult relationships. When the attachment is secure, the individual sees himself/herself as lovable and others as reliable and responsive to his/her needs. It is easy to trust.

If mothers were not responsive, then the child became insecurely or anxiously attached. Insecurely and anxiously attached individuals question whether they are lovable and whether others are reliable and responsive to their needs. It is hard to trust.

> **Instruct:** *Fill in the blanks from the information above.*
>
> [A securely attached person sees himself as LOVABLE and others as RELIABLE and RESPONSIVE to his needs.]
>
> [Share the process question.]

Instruct: Fill in the blank from the information above.

A securely attached person sees himself as L_____ and others as R_____ and R_____ to his needs.

Process Question: How can being insecurely attached cause problems in your relationships with women?

> **State:** *Here is another opportunity to read and learn about how our relationship with women is influenced by our mother.*
>
> [You can give the men an opportunity to read, but you should start and try to make the reading come alive. Also invite them to underline or mark anything that stands out to you.]

Mothering Styles

Parts of the following have been adapted from Dr. Susan Forward's 2002 book, The *Men Who Hate Women and the Women that Love them*, by Bantam Books.

The primary bond in a family is between the father and mother. When the father is missing, the primary bond becomes the mother and child. From this primary bond, unhealthy functioning in future relationships with women can result for the son if it is not properly balanced. We will refer to these bonds as different mothering styles. The mother's own fear or attempt to protect her child usually motivates these mothering styles.

The first is the overly close mothering style. This mother may inadvertently prevent her son's maturity. She does everything for him, but never cuts the umbilical cord that connects the two of them. The mother's motivation for this style is that the son may have taken the place of the absent father in the mother-father relationship. This can be seen in men who continue to stay with mothers as adults, or mothers who interfere in the relationship with the man's wife or significant other. When the son gets into a relationship with another woman, he may look for a mother rather than a wife. He may choose his mother over his wife.

A second style is the over-controlling mother. This type of mothering can create resentment in the son. This mother may be overcompensating for her son's lack of a father. She wants the best for her son but is excessively controlling in accomplishing it. She controls by being involved in too much detail, a critical attitude, or any type of abuse. This can create a foundation of resentment in relationships with women that result in a power struggle. The son attempts to use manipulation, abuse, or hatred to have the upper hand as he relates to women.

The third is the under-emotional mothering style. In this style, the mother has experienced victimization or rejects her son. This can create an intensive need to be mothered. This can be expressed through a man's excessive sex drive or the use of abuse to cover his vulnerability.[1]

Because mothers are important to children and men need women as well, we must learn how to have a respectable relationship with women. Understanding women and how your relationship with your mother can impact how you relate to women are important. This can help us to have healthy relationships with all the women in our lives.

> **Instruct:** *Fill in the blanks from the information above.*
>
> [Mothers who are overly close, over-controlling, or unavailable can adversely impact a son's ATTITUDE towards women.]

Instruct: Fill in the blank from the information above.

Mothers who are overly close, over-controlling, or not available can adversely impact a son's A_____ towards women.

> **State:** *Next we are going to discuss the process questions about our relationship with our mother and women and write down one thing we can do to improve our relationships with them. This includes our mother, sisters, daughters, and wife or significant other.*

Process Questions:

1. What kind of relationship did you have with your mother?
2. Was there something from this reading that spoke to you?
3. What have your relationships with women been like?
4. How can you apply what you learn to your relationships with women?

Instructions: From this section describe one thing you would like to improve your relationship with women.

_____

_____

_____

_____

3.2.b How to Treat a Woman

Relate To Her

> **State:** *In Shaunti Feldhahn's book (2006), For Men Only, she shares six key findings, based on a national scientific study, to give men the tools they need to love their wives the way they need to be loved.*
>
> **State:** *The information from this book can help improve all your relationships with the women in your life including your mother, sister, daughter, wife, or significant other.*

In Shaunti Feldhahn's book (2006), *For Men Only*, she shares six key findings, based on a national scientific study, to give men the tools they need to love their wives the way they need to be loved.

> **Instruct:** *Read the corresponding statement below and determine the word to insert into the blank to complete the statement.*
>
> [Answer key]
>   1. Reassure
>   2. Emotionally
>   3. Listen
>   4. Affirm
>   5. Time
>   6. Enjoy

Instructions: Read the corresponding statement below and determine the word to insert into the blank to complete the statement.

(Word Bank: Enjoy, Time, Affirm, Listen, Emotionally, Reassure)

1. R_____ her often of your love.
2. E_____ understand her to be a relief value.
3. L_____ to be a filter first and a fixer later.

4. A_____ her beauty as her mirror.
5. T_____ spent just being together.
6. E_____ the relationship and the differences.

> **State:** *The exercise we just completed can help you remember the six findings, and the following information can help us to better understand each finding.*

1. Many things that women do that frustrate men are often signals women need to be reassured that they are loved. The marriage deal is never really closed in her life after the ceremony. It is as if your wedding vows of "I do" mean to her an ongoing "Do you?" Share your love for her often.
2. Women may encounter frequent pop-ups of unresolved emotions and issues from the present and the past. When she has too much to carry and becomes overloaded and overwhelmed, she may need a venue to share what she feels. Men, you may need to learn to be comfortable with being uncomfortable with emotions, because she needs you.
3. Woman first want men to listen and validate how they feel about a problem before trying to fix it. Men often aren't aware of the need to take time to evaluate if the problem is emotional, and tend to immediately jump into fix mode. However, the emotion women experience is the real issue. They want those feelings to be heard and understood more than they want the problem solved.
4. In most if not all women, the little girl is still alive and well in them, and she needs to know her man thinks she's beautiful. Women are concerned about this every day, even if it is subconscious. A husband is a personal mirror that can choose to reflect to his wife the words of affirmation she's longing to hear. If we fail to do this, it leaves her in a fragile state, open to her own doubts and outside pressure from a hostile world. We can be a mirror or a hammer that can destroy everything.
5. Make one-on-one time together a priority. Make sure she knows you care for her first. You don't need to spend every minute outside of work with your wife, but make it clear that time together is a big priority to you. Show and share your commitment that you are there for her, no matter what. Staying away long hours to provide doesn't cut it when it hurts the very family for whom you are trying to provide. Be true partners in what goes on at home.
6. Enjoy knowing that, in the study, one of the most important thing women wanted their men to know was overwhelmingly, "You are my hero." They expressed how

much they admired, respected, and loved their husbands and wanted to make them happy. Many said how thankful they were for their wonderful husbands. In short, these women wanted their husbands to know they viewed their husbands as heroes. Nine out of ten women jumped at the chance to show how much they truly respect and appreciate their men. Enjoy your life with her!

> **Instruct:** *From this section describe one thing you can focus on doing more to fill your significant other's emotional tank.*

Instructions: From this section, describe one thing you can focus on doing more to fill your significant other's emotional tank.

_____

_____

_____

_____

_____

> **State:** *In his book* The Five Love Languages (2015), *Gary Chapman shares ways you can fill your spouse's or significant other's emotional love tank by speaking her specific love language. Please note that this also applies to your child, who also has a love language.*
>
> **Instruct:** *Match by drawing a line between the love language and description.*

Learn Her LOVE Language

Instructions: In his book *The Five Love Languages* (2015), Gary Chapman shares ways you can fill your spouse's emotional love tank by speaking her specific love language. Match by drawing a line between the love language and description.

1. Words of Affirmation	Nothing says, "I love you," like full, undivided attention. Being there for this type of person is critical, but really being there and putting everything else on hold makes your significant other feel truly special and loved. Distractions, postponed dates, or the failure to listen can be especially hurtful.

2. Acts of Service	This language isn't all about the bedroom. Hugs, pats on the back, holding hands, and thoughtful touches on the arm, shoulder, or face—they can all be ways to show excitement, concern, care, and love. Physical presence and accessibility are crucial, while neglect or abuse can be unforgivable and destructive.

3. Receiving Gifts	Actions don't always speak louder than words. If this is your love language, unsolicited compliments mean the world to you. Hearing the words, "I love you," is important—hearing the reasons behind that love sends your spirits skyward. Insults can leave you shattered and are not easily forgotten.

4. Quality Time	Can vacuuming the floors really be an expression of love? Absolutely! Anything you do to ease the burden of responsibilities weighing on an "Acts of Service" person will speak volumes. The words he or she most wants to hear are: "Let me do that for you." Laziness, broken commitments, and making more work for them tell speakers of this language their feelings don't matter.

5. Physical Touch	Don't mistake this love language for materialism; the receiver of gifts thrives on the love, thoughtfulness, and effort behind the gift. If you speak this language, the perfect gift or gesture shows that you are known, you are cared for, and you are prized above whatever was sacrificed to bring the gift to you. A missed birthday, anniversary, or a hasty, thoughtless gift would be disastrous—so would the absence of everyday gestures.

> **State:** *Knowing about love languages can give you some guidance on specific actions that can benefit your significant other. But how do you determine a person's love language?*
>
> **Instruct:** *We will review the following suggestions on determining your spouse's love language.*

How do you determine your love language? The following information can help you determine your love language.

1. Your upbringing can speak into your love language. How did your parents show you love growing up? What made you feel the most loved as a child? There is a high probability that is your primary love language.
2. When you really want to show someone you care about them, what first comes to your mind to show it? Your most basic instincts can show your primary love language as well.
3. Painful relational experiences can show your primary love language. If someone close to you hurt you in a deep way or neglected to show love the way you wanted, perhaps the deep hurt/dissatisfaction came because the way you most feel loved was not met. This means that what they failed to do is what you value the most, because it is your primary love language.

> **Instruct:** *Write down your significant other's love language and an example of why you think it fits.*

Instructions: From this section, describe what your significant other's love language is and share an example of why you think it fits.

3.3 Daddy Up

> rct 210 | rst 30 | est 15 | page 50
>
> **State:** *The role of a father is ultimately defined by the child. How well does the father take care of his child?*

The role of a father is ultimately defined by the child. It is all about what a father does to promote the well-being of his child. Defining child well-being includes different areas of development and need (Pollard & Lee, 2003). There are five areas of well-being that come from the research literature: 1) physical, 2) emotional, 3) social, 4) cognitive, and 5) economic (Pollard & Lee, 2003; Lippman, 2007; Bzostek, 2008). We will use these as we explore what children need and what dads do to fill those needs.

3.3.a What Your Child needs

> **State:** *The role of a father is ultimately defined by the child. How well does the father take care of his child?*
>
> **Instruct:** *Read the corresponding statement below and determine the word to insert into the blank to complete the statement.*
>
> [Answer Key]
>   1. Survival
>   2. Security
>   3. Support
>   4. Steering

Instructions: Choose from the following list to fill in the blanks.

Word Bank: [support, steer, security, survival]

1. Your child's physical needs involve their body and are critical to their _____ and growth.
2. Your child's emotional needs involve their feelings and are vital for their sense of _____ and belonging.
3. Your child's social needs involve their relationships and help strengthen their connections and _____ from others.
4. Your child's moral needs involve their behavior and _____ the choices they make in their conduct.

> **Instruct:** *Write down one example of a physical, emotional, social, and moral need.*
>
> [Possible examples]
> 1. Physical—Food, clothing, shelter, security, child support
> 2. Emotional—Love, identity, purpose, value, self-esteem, affirmation, intimacy, belonging, acceptance
> 3. Social—Relationship with parents, relationship with others, education, exercise, health care, nutrition, childcare
> 4. Moral—Values, spiritual, right and wrong, respect for authority, counsel and discipline

Instructions: Write down one example of physical, emotional, social, and moral need.

We need to be aware of our child's constant development. Their needs are also constantly changing, because of their growth. What was true of last week may not be true of this week.

Following is a beginning list of the types of needs and considerations we need to be aware of for our children. Our children have physical, cognitive, social, emotional needs along with milestones and problems to which we need to pay attention.

> **Note:** Keep in mind some men may not want or know how to read. You can choose to read the stages or ask for volunteers to read.
>
> **Instruct:** *Read through the developmental stages and particularly take note of the stage your child or children are in and their needs, milestones and potential problems.*

Instructions: Read through the developmental stages and particularly take note of the stage your child or children are in and their needs, milestones, and potential problems.

Infants and Toddlers

Physical

- Provide adequate nutrition, healthcare, and play with your child

Cognitive

- Interact with your child by holding them, giving them face time
- Back and forth responding to what they do and say

Social

- Spend time playing, reading, talking and taking care of them

Emotional

- Help form a secure attachment by being responsive to your child's need and comforting them

Milestones

- Walking, talking, mostly stable temperament and getting along with other children

Problems

- Malnutrition, lack of health care, rough treatment, lack of interaction and talking to them

Preschool

Physical

- Weight gain and height growth, gross and fine motor skills

Cognitive

- Need to grow in vocabulary, read many books

Social
- Cooperate with others and follow rules, know good from bad, exercise self-control

Emotional
- self-esteem based on what others tell him or her, less emotional outbursts, self-directed activities

Milestones
- Toilet-trained

Problems
- Social immaturity, anxiety or fear problems, lack of self-esteem or self-control, excessive aggression or tantrums, poor bladder control

School Age

Physical
- Slow, steady growth: 3-4 inches per year

Cognitive
- Recognize the perspective of others and the difference between behavior and intent

Social
- Friendships are situation-specific; begins to understand social roles and takes on more responsibilities at home

Emotional
- A self-esteem

Milestones
- Puberty begins from ages 10-12

Problems

- Emotional disturbances: depression, anxiety, PTSD, trust issues, abuse and neglect, bullying, experimentation with drugs and sex

Adolescents

Physical

- Growth spurt, puberty, bodies adjusting to growth spurt

Cognitive

- Can consider the consequences of thoughts and actions without experiencing them, considers the perspective of others, growth in thought and problem-solving

Social

- Distant from parents, identify more with peer group than parents, more independent

Emotional

- More self-conscience, developing and struggling with their own identity

Milestones

- Driving

Problems

- All the problems of school age: emotional disturbances, depression, anxiety, PTSD, trust issues, abuse and neglect, bullying, experimentation with drugs and sex

(Adapted from Rycus, 1998)

> **Instruct:** *Write down the needs you want to remember for your child, what they have been able to accomplish, and potential problems for which to be watchful.*

Instructions: Write down the needs you want to remember for your child, what they have been able to accomplish, and potential problems for which to be watchful.

_____

_____

_____

_____

_____

3.3.b What Dads Do

> **State:** *Men and women share many similarities and differences. While it may look different, women nurture and so do men—and nurturing is an important role of being a dad.*
>
> **Instruct:** *Read the corresponding statement below and determine the word to insert into the blank to complete the statement.*
>
> [Answer Key]
>   1. Providing, Protect, Discipline, Support
>   2. Time, Effort
>   3. Children
>   4. Develop

Men and women share many similarities and differences. While it may look different, women nurture and so do men—and nurturing is an important part of being a dad.

Children are love and care dependent. Just like a plant needs food, sun, soil, and water to grow and thrive our children need to be nurtured. Fathers help provide the nurture children need to grow and thrive.

Instructions: Using the following word bank to fill in the blanks.
(Time, Develop, Effort, Provide, Discipline, Protect, Children, Support)

1. Nurturing is P_____ for a child's needs, P_____ a child from harm, D_____ a child with healthy boundaries and S_____ a child to develop a healthy self-image.
2. Nurturing requires T_____ and E_____.
3. According to the research, nurturing is one of the most important variables in raising a healthy C_____.
4. Nurtured children D_____ to be competent, responsible, independent, confident, achievement-oriented, and able to control aggression and become healthy adults.

3.4 The Dad Plan

> rct 195 | rst 15 | est 15 | page 55
>
> **State:** *This section is one of the most important parts of the course, where you put knowledge into action.*
>
> **Instruct:** *Answer the following questions to create your Dad Plan to become a better dad. "I commit to maturing, respecting women, and serving others."*

Fathering Skill: Become a better dad by maturing as a man who respects women and serves others.

Remember to use SMART goals for your plan to turn your life around.

Instructions: Answer the following questions to create your Dad Plan to become a better dad.

1. What is my specific SMART (Specific, Measurable, Achievable, Realistic, Timetable) goal for growing in cultural awareness?

2. What can I do every day this week to grow more culturally aware?

3. When and where will I do this?

4. Who will hold me accountable?

4.0 Overcoming Challenges

rct 180 | rst 60 | est 15 | page 56

[Read the following.]

Warning: This section could be a trigger for some who have experienced first or second-hand trauma. Encourage participants: "Please feel free to take a break from the group if you need to, and make sure you take care of yourself today."

GOAL

To become a better dad,
I need healing from my past—
all the hurt, trauma and failures—
forgiving, making amends, and moving forward at last.

OBJECTIVES

1. Stable in Stress
2. The Trouble with Trauma
3. Healing through Forgiving, Making amends, and Moving On

The true measure of a father's desire for his children is noting what he allows to stop him from being a dad. The road of fatherhood has many obstacles that get in the way of us fathering our children. It takes a determined man to press through these challenges and be the dad his child needs.

Another way to look at the challenges in life is that they are stresses. A stress is a pressure we experience when we cannot cope with the demands of life.[2] These stresses divert our attention away from the task of being dad to that of dealing with the stress. Our time and effort is consumed by trying to relieve the stress. Often, because of the pressure, we can be pushed to make bad decisions in handling it.

4.1 Stable in Stress

> **State:** *In this next activity, we are going to test your building skills. Research shows the importance of stability in a child's environment and relationships. A father's stability is measured in his consistent presence, keeping his word, and maintaining a stable emotional state.*

Research shows the importance of stability in a child's environment and relationships. This is especially true for the relationship with a child's mother and father. A father's stability is measured in his consistent presence, keeping his word, and maintaining a stable emotional state.

4.1.a The Stress Test

> **Instruct:** *In this activity, the goal is to design and build a functioning bridge out of index cards (3x5) that can support the weight of a water bottle. The bridge must be at least 1 inch high x 3 inches wide x 5 inches long. You can use up to six index cards to build your bridge.*
>
> **State:** *The two building tips are: 1. one card is for the top surface, and 2. the other is that triangles help make any structure stronger.*

Instructions: In this activity, the goal is to design and build a functioning bridge out of index cards (3x5) that can support the weight of a water bottle. The bridge must be at least 1 inch high x 3 inches wide x 5 inches long. You can use up to six index cards to build your bridge.

Here are two building tips:

1. Use one card for the top surface.
2. Triangles help make any structure stronger.

> [Share the process questions.]

Process Questions:
1. Why was your bridge able or unable to support the weight of the water bottle?
2. How can you compare this exercise to our ability to handle stress or drama?
3. What are the consequences of not being able to handle stress or drama?

4.1.b What Is Stress?

> **Ask:** *How do you define stress?*
>
> **State:** *Let's read the definition of stress.*

4.1 Stress is the daily pressures a man experiences that can impact his functioning, that results from the idea there is a lack of resources to address differing intensities, frequencies, and durations of life demands.

> **State:** *Not all stress is bad; sometimes stress can help us grow and develop. Next, we will look at the three common classifications of stress.*
>
> **Instruct:** *I will read the definition of each type of stress and give you a minute to write down three examples of that type of stress. You will then have a chance to share your examples.*

Not all stress is bad; sometimes stress can help us grow and develop. Next, we will look at the three common classifications of stress (CWIG, 2015; NSCDC, 2007).

Instructions: Write down three examples of stress for each of the types of stress.

> [Answer Key]
> 1. Positive stress: meeting new people, going to the dentist, dealing with frustration and discipline
> 2. Tolerable stress: the death of a loved one, divorce, natural disaster, frightening injury
> 3. Toxic stress: chronic neglect, caregiver mental illness or substance abuse, exposure to violence

1. Positive stress is moderate and short-lived, causing brief increases in heart rate or mild changes in stress hormone levels. Learning to adjust to this type of stress is an important and necessary aspect of healthy development that occurs in the context of stable and supportive relationships (CWIG, NSCDC).
   a. _____
   b. _____
   c. _____
2. Tolerable stress is severe enough to disrupt brain architecture if unchecked, but is buffered by supportive relationships that facilitate adaptive coping and mitigate the damaging effects (CWIG, NSCDC). Tolerable stress generally occurs within a time-limited period, which gives the brain an opportunity to recover from potentially damaging effects.
   a. _____
   b. _____
   c. _____
3. Toxic stress is that which is severe and prolonged in the absence of the buffering protection of supportive relationships. Toxic stress disrupts brain architecture and leads to lifelong problems in learning, behavior, and both physical and mental health (CWIG, NSCDC). Relationships can mitigate the toxicity of stress.
   a. _____
   b. _____
   c. _____

4.1.c The Impact of Stress

> **State:** *How might stress affect the way a father functions in his role? Let's look at a model that illustrates how stress may impact a father.*
>
> [Read the following.]

The Child FIRST model is a way to illustrate the impact of a father's life stressors on how he functions in his role as a father. In the model, a father's role is represented by a simple machine. The father is the fulcrum and his functioning is the lever. His functioning points to his involvement, which can range from healthy to unhealthy.

Child-FIRST Model

Child-Father Involvement Resource/Stress Theoretical Model

(Williams, 2016)

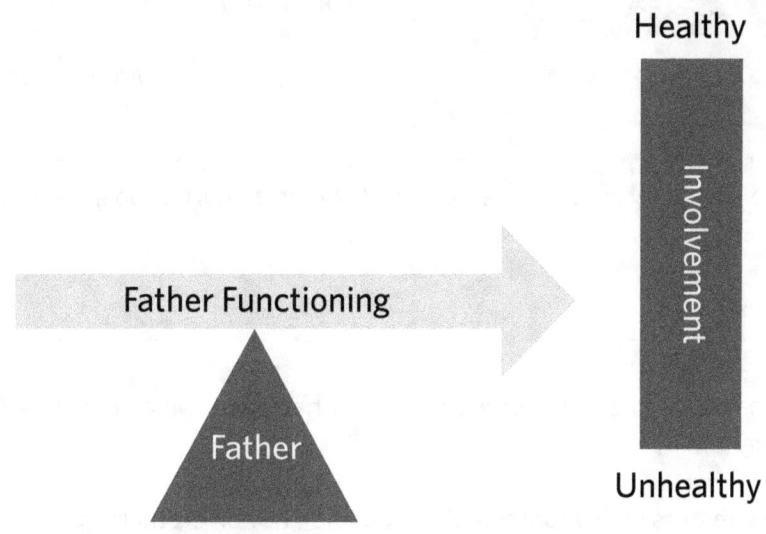

(Williams, 2016)

Process Question: How many fathers do you think are functioning with healthy involvement?

Stressors are the daily pressures a man experiences that can impact his functioning, that result from the idea there is a lack of resources to address differing intensities, frequencies, and durations of life demands.

Child-FIRST Model

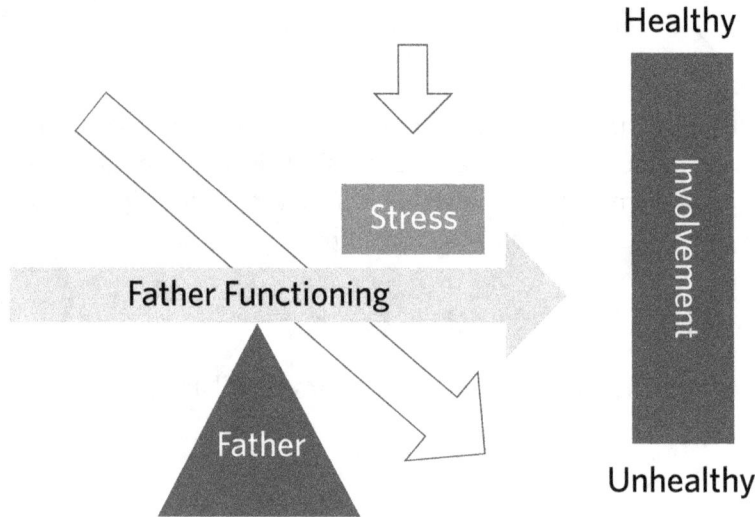

(Williams, 2016)

> **Note:** If you have the capability, write the responses down on a chart or board to refer to later.]
>
> [Ask the process questions.]

Process Question: What are some of the stressors that fathers face, which may interfere with his role as a father?

When fathers face life stressors or environmental risk factors, they divert their limited time, attention, and resources to address those stressors or risks and leave less time, attention, and resources to focus on the needs of the child. These stressors pile up on top of each other.

Child-FIRST Model

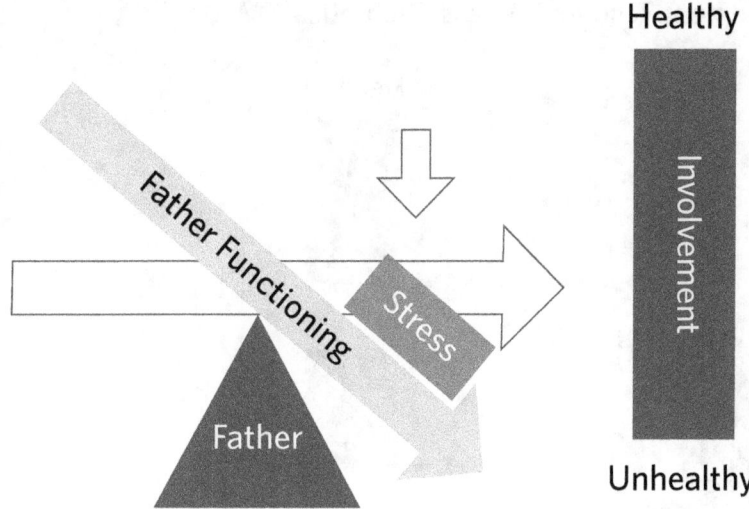

Process Questions: Give examples of how and why stressors can divert a father's attention to fathering.

While in many cases, stress cannot be eliminated, it can be counter balanced, with resources to address the stressors. Notice that sometimes the resources can be a positive stressor for a time, but later result in relief. And one of the biggest resources is other people in stable supportive relationships.

Child-FIRST Model
Child-(Father Involvement Resource/Stress Theoretical) Model

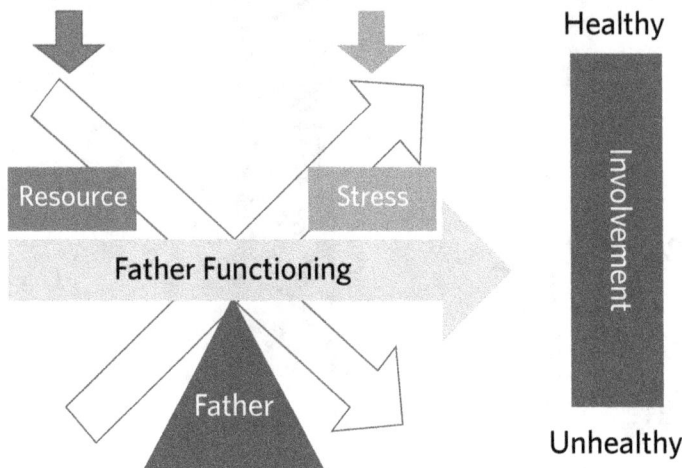

Process Questions:

1. Pair the stressors we came up with earlier with a resource that can help eliminate the stress.
2. What ways can fathers be supported to decrease stressors?
3. What ways can fathers be supported to increase resources?
4. Why don't fathers get the help they need?
5. How can we help get fathers to a place where they will seek and accept help?

The reasons for father absence are diverse and complex. Regardless of the reason for the absence or withdrawal of social capital, the question arises as to the impact that withdrawal on the child. Research links father absence with a host of negative social outcomes for children.

Everyone experiences stress to varying degrees and durations. However, not everyone has adequate resources to handle the stressors they face. For these people, the perception of stressors can pile up into constant crises that hamper their functioning in life.

4.1 Stress can be a barrier to being a good father or, in the context of resources and stable support, can challenge us to develop and improve our role as a man and father.

4.2 The Trouble with Trauma

> rct 165 | rst 45 | est 15 | page 62
>
> **State:** *If your parents divorced, what does that have to do with your risk of heart disease as an adult? If your father had a drinking problem, are you more likely to suffer from depression?*
>
> **State:** *Next, you are going to receive information that may save or prolong your life. We will look at the link of adverse childhood experiences to later negative adult health outcomes.*

What does a child's parents' divorce have to do with their risk of heart disease as an adult? If a child's father had a drinking problem, is he more likely to suffer from depression? The linking of adverse childhood experiences to later negative adult health outcomes has been said to be one of the most significant public health issues.

4.2.a Cuts Like a Knife

> [Read the definition of trauma.]

Trauma is defined as an inescapable horrendous experience(s) that overwhelms coping. It traps a person in the experiences(s)—body, brain, and behavior—and can cut the person off from healthy relating to self, children, and others.

State: *To better understand emotional trauma, we will compare the similarities to physical trauma.*

Instruct: *Write down the ways a physical wound is similar to a heart or emotional wound.*

[Answer Key]
1. Visible
2. Painful
3. Don't Ignore
4. Cleaning
5. Infection
6. Medication
7. Flies
8. Takes time
9. Scar

Instructions: Write down the ways a physical wound is like a heart or emotional wound.

Physical Wound	Heart Wound
1	1
2	2
3	3
4	4
5	5

[Read the following and ask the process questions.]

There are three characteristics of people who have experienced emotional trauma. Following is a list:

1. Reliving the heart wound
2. Avoiding things that remind you of the heart wound
3. Alarms are constantly going off for you

Process questions:

1. Do you know people who have experienced one of these characteristics?
2. What is an example of reliving the heart wound?
3. What is an example of how someone might avoid the reminders of the heart wound?
4. What is an example of someone who is constantly on edge?
5. How might these three emotional trauma characteristics affect you personally?

4.2.a The ACE Study

> **State:** *Next, we are going to look at the Adverse Childhood Experiences Study to learn about the impact of trauma.*
>
> [Read the following.]

The ACE Study. In late 1990s, an epidemiologist, Dr. Robert Anda, and preventative medicine doctor, Dr. Vincent Felitti, led a collaborative study between the Centers for Disease Control and Prevention (CDC) and Kaiser Permanente to assess the association between childhood experiences and lifelong health (Felitti et al., 1998). An adverse childhood experience (ACE) is an extremely stressful event that can actually alter brain development and the immune system. The Adverse Childhood Experience Study (ACES) surveyed 17,337 adults for 10 types of childhood trauma and found associations between these adverse childhood experiences and later-life health and well-being outcomes (Felitti et al., 1998).

The Results. Five of the types of childhood trauma are personal, and five are household dysfunction. The findings from the ACE Study suggest that experiences of childhood trauma are major risk factors for the leading causes of illness and death, as well as poor quality of life. The majority (67%) of the largely white, middle class, college-educated respondents with good health insurance experienced trauma, citing:

- 28 percent had been physically abused
- 27 percent experienced household substance abuse
- 23 percent had divorced parents
- 21 percent were sexually abused
- 17 percent had household members with mental illness
- 13 percent had witnessed household domestic violence
  (Felitti et al., 1998)

> **State:** *One of the two key findings in this study is how incredibly common ACE experiences occur.*

Adverse Childhood Experiences

Abuse	Neglect	Household Dysfunction
Physical	Physical	Mental Illness
Emotional	Emotional	Incarceration
Sexual		Mother Treated Violently
		Divorce
		Substance Abuse

Associated Outcomes

Behavior				
Lack of Physical Activity	Smoking	Alcoholism	Drug Use	Missed Work
Physical & Mental				
Severe Obesity	Diabetes	Depression	Suicide Attempts	STDs
Heart Disease	Cancer	Stroke	COPD	Broken Bones

(Centers for Disease Control and Prevention, 2016)

4.2.b The Ace Survey

> **Warn:** *Warning, this survey could be a trigger for some who have experienced first or second-hand trauma. Please feel free to take a break from the group if you need to, and make sure you take care of yourself today.*
>
> **State:** *Next, we will personalize the ACE score to gain a deeper understanding of it, but don't worry, you will not be asked to share the number.*
>
> **Instruct:** *Read through the quiz below, and answer the questions as honestly as possible by making a mental note of an "X" in the Yes column. Please do not mark your actual answer in this book for confidentiality purposes.*
>
> [Read the survey questions and give time for the men think about their responses.]

This next activity will give us the experience of reviewing the ACE Survey and understanding what participants were answering to get their scores. This will also give us insight into our own childhood. **Please note you will not write down your score.**

Instructions: Read through the quiz below, and answer the questions as honestly as possible by making a mental note of an "X" in the Yes column. **Please do not mark your actual answer in this book for confidentiality purposes.**

While you were growing up, during your first 18 years of life:	Y
1. Did your parent or other adult in your household **often or very often** . . . Swear at you, insult you, put you down or humiliate you? **OR** act in a way that made you afraid that you might be physically hurt?	
2. Did a parent or other adult in the household **often or very often** . . . push, grab, slap or throw something at you? **OR** ever hit you so hard that you had marks or were injured?	
3. Did an adult or person at least 5 years older than you **ever** . . . touch or fondle you or have you touch their body in a sexual way? **OR** attempt or actually have oral, anal, or vaginal intercourse with you?	

4. Did you **often or very often** feel that . . . no one in your family loved you or thought you were important or special? **OR** your family didn't look out for each other, feel close to each other or support each other?	
5. Did you **often or very often** feel that . . . you didn't have enough to eat, had to wear dirty clothes, and had no one to protect you? **OR** your parents were too drunk or high to take care of you or take you to the doctor if you needed it?	
6. Was a biological parent **ever** lost to you through divorce, abandonment, or other reasons?	
7. Was your mother or stepmother **often or very often** pushed, grabbed, slapped, or had something thrown at her? **OR sometimes, often or very often** kicked, bitten, hit with a fist, or hit with something hard? **OR ever** repeatedly hit for at least a few minutes or threatened with a gun or knife?	
8. Did you live with anyone who was a problem drinker or alcoholic or who used street drugs?	
9. Was a household member depressed or mentally ill **OR** did a household member attempt suicide?	
10. Did a household member go to prison?	
Total number of Yeses	

(Felitti et al., 1998)

Instruct: *Total the number of Yes responses. This is your ACE score. It is for you to personally contemplate. Please do not share with others.*

[Ask the process questions.]

Instructions: Total the number of Yes responses. This is your ACE score. It is for you to personally contemplate. Please do not share with others.

Process Questions
1. What was the experience of taking this quiz for you?
2. What do you think the clients experience in taking this quiz?
3. Was anybody surprised by the results?
4. What should be our response to taking this survey?

> **Note:** Because we are not using their real ACE score, they need to be randomly assigned a score. Either you can have each person roll a dice, or you can do the exercise below.
>
> **Instruct:** *Pick a number from 1 to 10 and write that number in the box below.*

Instructions: For the next exercise, pick a number between 1 and 10 and write that number in the box below.

[Read the following]

"We are not a score, but a score can give insight to help us overcome."
(Williams, 2017)

The Impact of Trauma

Research that nationally estimated exposure to traumatic events found that 89.7% of those surveyed had experienced one or more traumatic events (Kilpatrick, et al., 2013). Based on the weighting of the sample, there is some ability to generalize the findings to the population of U.S. adults. This study supports that most adults have experienced some type of trauma.

> **State:** *The second key finding is the strong relationship between having ACEs and having your life shortened by health and well-being problems.*

The second key finding of the ACEs study is the strong relationship between the number of ACEs and later life-threatening health issues. The following is a table illustrating the relationship:

1.	0 ACEs	Normal risks	All other scores compared to
2.	1 ACE	2x more likely	Alcoholic, Substance Abuser, Suicide
3.	2 ACEs	4x more likely 3x more likely 2x more likely	Alcoholic, Substance Abuser Suicide STD, Depressed
4.	3 ACEs	7x more likely 5x more likely 3x more likely 2x more likely	Attempt Suicide Alcoholic, Substance Abuser Depressed Chronic Bronchitis or Emphysema
5.	4 ACEs or more	12x more likely 7x more likely 4x more likely 3x more likely 2x more likely	Attempt Suicide Alcoholic, Substance Abuser Bronchitis or Emphysema, Depressed Heart Disease, Stroke, Cancer Hepatitis, Poor Health, Diabetes
7.	6 ACEs or more	Live 20 years less	Earlier Death

(Felitti et al., 1998)

> **State:** *Next, we will look at how these adverse childhood experiences may have shaped your role as a father.*

The experiences that happened to you as a child shape who you become as a father. All fathers were once sons. This is a reminder that many fathers who may have experienced trauma were once sons. Many fathers may have experienced trauma as sons that have never been resolved.

Instructions: Use the following word bank and choose the right word for each statement.

Word Bank: **behavioral, mood, self-concept, attachment**

1. Fathers who were exposed to trauma as children may have experienced the uncertain and unpredictable environment that can contribute to _____ problems that result in distrust, suspicion, isolation, and relationship trouble.
2. Fathers who were exposed to trauma as children may have experienced a _____ that is unstable, have low self-esteem, distorted body image, and strong feelings of shame and guilt.
3. Fathers who were exposed to trauma as children may have had trouble regulating their _____, as well as knowing what they want and feel and struggling to communicate it with others.
4. Fathers who were exposed to trauma as children may exhibit poor _____ control, have self-destructive behavior, aggression, and sleep and eating disorders.

4.3 Healing, Forgiving, Making Amends, and Moving on

---

rct 150 | rst 30 | est 15 | page 69

Ask: *How do we begin to move past these traumatic experiences?*

State: *Our next activity may give us insight to the answer to this question.*

4.3.a Dice Activity: 2 Steps Forward, 3 Steps Back

Dice Activity: 2 Steps Forward, 3 Steps Back

Instructions: You will roll five die to match the three patterns in the order they appear. You may save the numbers you roll, or re-roll as many times are you need. However, if you roll any "1" or "6" you must re-roll all the die. (Williams, 2010)

1. Four of the same number.
   example

3	3	3	3

2. Four numbers in sequence.
   example

2	3	4	5

3. Two different pairs.
   example

2	2	4	4

Process questions:

1. What made this activity so challenging?
2. Can you think of any way to guard against this challenge?
3. How might challenges fathers face bring them back to a place where they feel they are starting all over?

4.3.b Feel Like Giving Up?

Ask: *Did you feel like giving up?*

State: *Some participants have been so frustrated with the previous exercise that they gave up. When we make efforts to move forward and keep being held back or taken back further it can lead to giving up. The following story illustrates this point.*

Learned Helplessness

Seligman and Maier (1967) were doing research on classical conditioning, or the process by which an animal or human associates one thing with another. In the case of Seligman's experiment, he would ring a bell and then give a light shock to a dog. After several times, the dog reacted to the shock even before it happened: as soon as the dog heard the bell, he reacted as though he'd already been shocked.

But, then something unexpected happened. Seligman put each dog into a large crate that was divided down the middle with a low fence. The dog could see and jump over the fence if necessary. The floor on one side of the fence was electrified, but not on the other side of the fence. Seligman put the dog on the electrified side and administered a light shock. He expected the dog to jump to the non-shocking side of the fence.

Instead, the dogs lay down. It was as though they'd learned from the first part of the experiment that there was nothing they could do to avoid the shocks, so they gave up in the second part of the experiment. In a follow-up experiment, dogs who were not previously exposed to shocks quickly jumped the fence to escape the shocks.

Seligman described their condition as learned helplessness, or not trying to get out of a negative situation, because the past has taught you that you are helpless.

We must consider the experiences that people go through and learn how it shapes them and their responses. Some people have learned to be helpless and it is not easy to change. Next, we will look at how a father wound and incarceration may be traumatic barriers to fathering.

State: *The biological father and mother are potentially the two most influential people in the life of their child. Mothers and fathers contribute an emotional significance that can profoundly help or hurt their child. Sometimes this is true whether they are present, absent, good, or bad. The father and mother influence is biologically through genetics, bio-socially through epigenetics or life experiences that can express or suppress genes which can be inherited by their children, and socially through social experiences.*

The Father Wound

In this course, we have viewed the Amos story about the wounds of an absent father and we have been made aware of the number of children growing up absent their biological father. The emotional wounding or trauma an absent father may inflict on his son may cause problems in the son's future relationship with his child. There are three related experiences as a son which, together or alone, may become a challenge to a man's own role as a father. Those experiences are: emotionally needing something from your father you were denied, lacking the presence of a healthy father role model, and being a victim of abuse by your father.

When you are a child, you are not likely to have the resources or capacity to resolve the wounds or trauma. Growing up to be men in American culture, we are taught to handle our own problems, so we learn to suppress our problems. Many men are reluctant to cry in our culture. Even though everyone says it is okay for men to cry, we don't often enough and instead learn to suppress our emotions. We are usually okay if no one brings up or talks about the issue. As a result, many men still have unresolved issues with their fathers. One of the most effective paths to healing for these men is the process of forgiveness.

Process Questions:

1. How might a father wound be a factor is in a man's own father absence?
2. How can you help someone identify this issue in his own life?
3. How would a person get help?
4. How might the information in this section help your work with families?
5. Process statement: Trauma is the unseen enemy that can sabotage the success of the father unless it is recognized and addressed.

> **State:** *When a child is ripped from his or her family and placed in the foster care system, no matter how well intended the providers, it is a traumatic experience for a child. For many men who are separated from their children through divorce, a hostile relationship, or incarceration, it can be traumatic for fathers.*

Incarceration

In 2008, more than half (1.2 million) of the 2.3 million people who were incarcerated in U.S. prisons or jails were parents of children ages 18 and younger (The Pew Charitable

Trusts, 2010). Nine out of 10 incarcerated parents were fathers of an estimated 2.7 million children who had a parent incarcerated in 2008 (The Pew Charitable Trusts). Incarcerated parents deal with separation and loss issues of their children. Visitation and other contacts help them to deal with these issues and to develop and maintain their role as parents (Lincroft, 2011). Research has shown that, if incarcerated fathers maintain contact with their children, they are less likely to recidivate (Lincroft). An incarcerated father's regular visits with his child is an important first step forward in the family reunification process (Lincroft).

The children also benefit from the contact by being able to process the emotional reaction of separation, to have a more realistic understanding of their father's circumstance, and be assured they are not to blame and their father will be safe (Lincroft). Research showed that when fathers are incarcerated, their children may show increases in externalizing behavior problems that are directed toward others, such as aggression, violence, or delinquency. There may also be increases in internalizing behavior problems that are directed inward such as depression, anxiety, and difficulty paying attention (Johnson, 2009; Wakefield, 2011). Another study reported a strong association between paternal incarceration and increases in mental and physical problems in young adults, including depression, PTSD, anxiety, high cholesterol, asthma, and overall health problems (Lee, Fang, & Luo, 2013).

Process Questions

1. Why is it important to stay in contact with your child even when incarcerated?
2. What are things you can do to stay in contact?
3. How can a father improve his situation while incarcerated?

4.3.c Forgiveness and Moving Forward

> **Ask:** *How do I know if I need to forgive my father?*
>
> **State:** *We can take the non-scientific fathering history survey that can provide some insight to whether you may have a father wound.*
>
> [Take time to read the instructions and make sure everyone understands.]

Fathering History Survey

Instructions: Evaluate each statement by marking a number that reflects your response, where 5 means strongly agree and 1 means strongly disagree. Follow the instructions to determine your total score and what your score suggests.

Group 1					
1. My father was supportive of me.	1	2	3	4	5
2. It was easy to get close to my father.	1	2	3	4	5
3. As a child, I knew what my father felt about me.	1	2	3	4	5
4. My father regularly showed his affection for me.	1	2	3	4	5
5. My father was a good example.	1	2	3	4	5
Total					
Group 2					
1. My father used alcohol or drugs often.	1	2	3	4	5
2. My father was mostly absent during my childhood.	1	2	3	4	5
3. My father abused me or another family member.	1	2	3	4	5
4. My father was sexually unfaithful to my mother.	1	2	3	4	5
5. My father was convicted of a crime or committed illegal acts.	1	2	3	4	5
Total					
Group 3					
1. I read parenting literature often.	1	2	3	4	5
2. I have a close friend who supports me.	1	2	3	4	5
3. I am regularly involved in a small group.	1	2	3	4	5
4. I keep in contact with my kids frequently.	1	2	3	4	5
5. I am seeking ways to improve/strengthen my parenting.	1	2	3	4	5
Total					

(Williams, 2010)

OVERCOMING CHALLENGES

(Group 1 Total) _____ **subtracted from**
(Group 2 Total) _____

Sub-Total _____ **added to**

(Group 3 Total) _____

Total Score _____

Results Range −15 to +45

Strong Heritage	34–45
Solid Foundation	33–19
Challenged Position	18–7
Wounded Heart	−15–6

Process Questions

1. How might your own history with your father or the father of your children influence your attitudes and behaviors towards other fathers?
2. What are ways you can prevent this from happening?

> **Ask:** *What is forgiveness and what is it not?*
>
> **State:** *One of the challenges with forgiveness is that a misunderstanding about forgiveness makes it more difficult, if not impossible, to give.*
>
> [Take time to read the instructions and make sure everyone understands.]

Instructions: In the first column, write down what forgiveness is not. In the second column, write down what forgiveness is.

What forgiveness is not	What forgiveness is

Forgiveness is a process and choice you have the power to make. You can grant forgiveness to someone who may not deserve it, or ask for it and free yourself from the offense. This can start you on the road to healing.

State: *Writing a forgiveness letter can be helpful to move you along the process of forgiveness. Through the letter, you have a chance in a safe environment of writing to explore the pain, ask questions, share your sorrow, and position yourself to forgive.*

State: *Remember forgiveness is NOT about releasing someone from the consequences of their actions, restoring trust, saying it was okay to offend, waiting for the hurt to stop, or being cheap.*

Forgiveness Letter

Instructions: Write down a forgiveness letter

1. Name the wound
2. Write down your worst pain
3. Share it with someone
4. Destroy the letter

4.4 The Dad Plan

> rct 135 | rst 15 | est 15 | page 75
>
> **State:** *This section is one of the most important parts of the course, where you put knowledge into action.*
>
> **Instruct:** *Answer the following questions to create your dad plan to heal from your past through forgiveness and lower your stress.*

Fathering Skill: Become a better dad by healing from my past through forgiveness and lowering stress and moving forward.

Remember to use SMART goals for your plan to turn your life around.

Instructions: Answer the following questions to create your dad plan to become a better dad.

1. What is my specific SMART (Specific, Measurable, Achievable, Realistic, Timetable) goal for growing in cultural awareness?
2. What can I do every day this week to grow more culturally aware?
3. When and where will I do this?
4. Who will hold me accountable?

5.0 Becoming Dad

> rct 120 | rst 60 | est 15 | page 76
>
> [Read the following]

GOAL

To become a better dad,
I will be humble and seek to learn
ways to improve as a parent, co-parent, and citizen,
and let this passion be a better burn.

OBJECTIVES

1. Better relational skills
2. Better co-parenting Skills
3. Better fathering Skills

To be the best dad, we need to stand up against myths that will get in the way of our growth and development as a father. One myth is that we are an island and can do it all alone. No man is an island; we were created for relationships and in the context of relationships we grow and develop. We need others and others need us.

Another myth is we know all we need to know about being a father. There are no perfect fathers; we all have room to learn. Although *Becoming Dads* is a solid program, it is just scratching the surface of all that is available to learn on this lifelong journey of fatherhood.

The best way to take advantage of all that is to be humble and open to learning from others in their successes and failures, from the young and old, strangers and family, and the list goes on. We even learn from our own children. Are you ready to be better?

5.1 Better Relational Skills

> **State:** *Learning to relate to others begins in our family. Next, we are going to look back to reflect on life in our family: what worked, what didn't work and what needs to be improved.*
>
> [Read the following, give instructions on activity, and share process questions.]

5.1.a The Family Tree

A genogram is a graphical representation of a person's family relationships. In this exercise, we will develop a simple genogram to write about the parents you spent the most time with as a child.

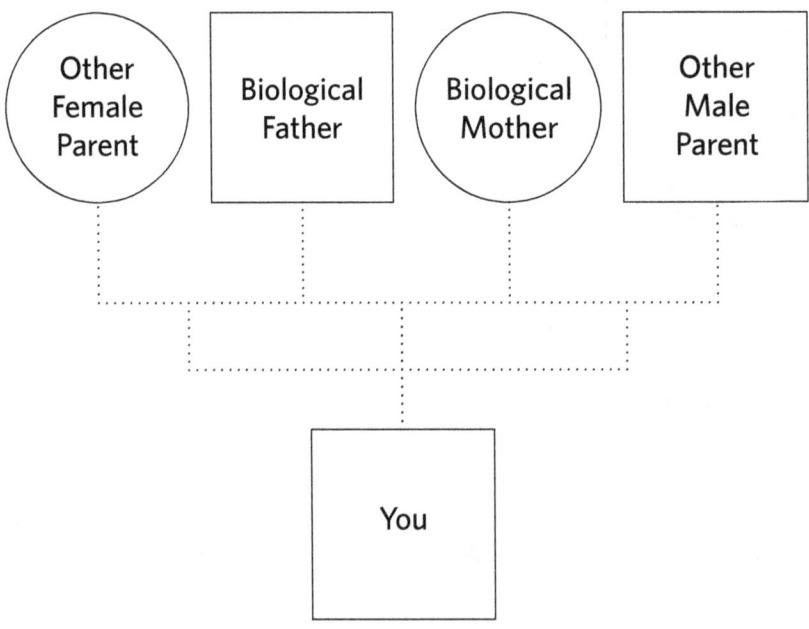

Instructions: Complete the following actions.

1. If you know it, write the name of your biological father and mother above their box.
2. Draw over the dotted lines to connect the two parents you spent the most time living with, to each other (whether with both biological parents or one biological parent and their partner).
3. If one of your "parents" was a partner of your biological parent, write that name above the shape.
4. Draw over dotted lines to connect the two parents to you.

Process Questions:

1. Were your "parents" married; if not, did it matter to you?
2. Describe what your relationship was like with your father and/or your other male parent.
3. Describe your relationship with your mother or your other female parent.
4. How did your parents' relationship (or parents' partnering relationships) impact you?
5. Describe the things you liked about your family.
6. Describe the things you did not like about your family.
7. What would you change for your family?

5.1.b Family Needs

> **Ask:** *What are the most basic needs of a family?*
>
> **State:** *Everyone in the family needs to be known, have a strong sense of belonging, and have their needs met or fulfilled. This includes you and the children.*
>
> [Read the following, give the instructions ,and do the activity.]

Being Known

Using a cognitive and behavior perspective to Maslow's Hierarchy of Needs, Ryan and Deci argue there are three basic or core innate psychological needs, which are described as competence, relatedness, and autonomy. From the study of this theory, Dr. Henriques suggests you can go further by identifying the need an individual has to be known and valued by self and important to others.

Being "known" means that the individual is able to share their full experiences, private thoughts, and public image with important others. It can be considered the single most important variable in human development in terms of outcomes regarding character structure and well-being.

Instructions: What do you know about your child? Here are questions we need to ask our child regularly, because they often change. Write your answer to the question in the space provided. As a take-home assignment, find out your child's answers to the questions to see how many you get right.

Awareness Quiz

1. What is your child's favorite color?

Your answer	Your child's answer

2. Who is your child's best friend?

Your answer	Your child's answer

3. What is your child's favorite game?

Your answer	Your child's answer

4. What is your child's favorite movie or TV show?

Your answer	Your child's answer

5. What is your child's favorite food, drink, dessert, or candy?

Your answer	Your child's answer

6. What is your child's favorite song?

Your answer	Your child's answer

7. What is your child's favorite book?

Your answer	Your child's answer

8. What does your child want to be when he/she grows up?

Your answer	Your child's answer

Your child's wants to be known by you, so study your child.

Belonging

Another core family need is the need we possess to belong. Attachment theory explores the deep and enduring emotional bond that connects one person to another across time and space (Bowlby, 1969).

We are born love and care dependent, and throughout life have a need for important others. The others refer to those people the individual cares about and usually includes: 1) family of origin, 2) present family, 3) romantic partners/interests, 4) close friends, 5) peers, and 6) social identities/group affiliations.

Process Question: How can you show your child that he/she has a place to belong with you, especially if you do not live in his or her home?

Being Fulfilled

Being valued in a family means that one is prized, admired, and/or loved, and that one's interests are respected and honored. It naturally follows that the family members would be provided care and the meeting of their needs.

In the McMaster's model of family functioning, Epstein, Bishop, and Baldwin (1984), share the model's stated assumptions about the primary function of the family is to provide a setting for the development and maintenance of family members on a biological, social, and psychological level. The functioning of the family is grouped into three areas: the basic tasks, developmental tasks, and crisis tasks.

Being fulfilled is having all the three tasks of the family fulfilled:

- the basic task of the family member being provided items such as food, clothing, money, transportation, and housing
- the developmental task of fostering healthy growth through all the developmental life cycle
- the hazardous tasks of handling crises within the family due to internal or external factors

Fatherhood is about providing for the needs of our child physically, emotionally, socially, and spiritually.

5.1.c Speaking

State: *One of the two foundational skills that can help us meet the needs of children to be known, to belong, and to be fulfilled is speaking. Let's start by reviewing the sayings related to speaking and words to determine if they hold true today.*

[Share the instructions.]
[Answer key: Note someone may reason for a different answer.]
1. False
2. True
3. True
4. False
5. True

Instructions: Review the sayings on speaking and words and determine if they hold true today.

1. "Sticks and stones may break my bones, but words will never harm me."
2. "Be slow to speak and quick to listen."
3. "No words can help you more or hurt you more than the words spoken by your biological parents."
4. "Children should be seen, but not heard."
5. "The power of life and death is in the tongue."
6. "Loose lips sink ships."
7. "Out of the abundance of the heart the mouth speaks."

Ask: *So, what are the things about speaking we should know?*

Instructions: *Read the following statements and determine which word from the word bank best fits in the blank.*

[Answer Key]
1. **Think**
2. **Known**
3. **Know**
4. **Build**
5. **Blaming and Criticizing**
6. **Body Language**
7. **Open-ended**—often begin with why, how, what, and who, maybe, request, describe for me . . . , tell me about . . . , what do you think about . . . These can help your child weigh options; be sure to avoid being judgmental.

Instructions: Read the following statements and determine which word from the word bank best fits in the blank.

1. It is important that you _____ about what you want before you speak.
2. A goal of speaking is to be _____, who you are, and what you want and need.
3. Another goal of speaking to _____ others, who they are, and what they want and need.

4. Another important reason we speak is to B_____ others up and not tear them down.
5. We should avoid _____ and _____ others.
6. Make sure what you say aligns with your _____.
7. _____ questions encourage a full, meaningful answer from your child's own thoughts and feelings that help you know them better.

Process Questions:

1. Did your parents speak to you in demeaning ways?
2. Did people speak things into your life that built you up?
3. What words have been spoken to you in the past that still affect you today?
4. What's wrong with this statement, "I just don't understand my child; he doesn't listen to me."?

5.1.d Listening

"Listening to someone's thoughts and feelings affirms their self-worth." —grw

> **State:** *The other foundational skills that can help us meet the needs of children to be known, to belong, and to be fulfilled is listening. Let's review a few things about listening.*

When you LISTEN, you must be quiet first, then you should say what you hear the other person say. The goal of listening is to understand the other person.

> **State:** *How important are words, sounds, and body language in communication?*
>
> [Share the instructions and ask the process question.]

Instructions: Communication can be divided into three components that comprise it. Write in what percent of communication are words, sounds, and body language.

Words	Sounds	Body Language	Total
%	%	%	100%

Process Question: What does this tell you about communication?

> **Ask:** *What does it mean to listen?*
>
> **State:** *In the next exercise, we will look at the depth of the meaning of listening.*
>
> [Share the instructions and ask the process question.]

Instructions: Take 30 seconds and fill in the blanks for the different aspects of listening in the word "Ting" from the following list: Heart, Attention, Eyes, Body, Mind, and Ears.

Ting (traditional Chinese word for Listen)
1. To hear (twice as much as you speak)
2. To think (being in the moment)
3. To be present (be there)
4. To see (face to face)
5. To focus (not distracted by other things)
6. To feel (empathy)

Reflective listening involves paying respectful attention to the content and feelings of your child to let them know that they were heard and understood by sharing it back.
   The reflecting skills involve the following:

1. Non-verbal gestures and brief one or two-word statements that you are listening.
2. Reflecting the content of the essence of what was said in your own words.
3. Reflecting the feelings to the others in your own words.

Instructions: In the first scenario, the facilitator will play the role of the child who does the talking and the father who uses reflective listening in the first scenario. In the second scenario, you will pair up and take turns being the father and child so you can practice reflective listening.

1. Child: "You always fight with mom. Why can't you get along with her? When you both raise your voices and yell at each other and say bad things, I get scared something bad is going to happen. I love you both. I wish you would stop."
2. Child: "You promised you were coming to pick me up yesterday and you didn't. I was waiting and waiting for you and you never came. I cried all afternoon. Mommy said, something must have come up. But why didn't you even call? I don't believe you anymore. You can't even do what you say you are going to do."

Process Question: How do you think reflective listening can be helpful in your relationship with your child and others?

5.2 Co-Parenting

> rct 105 | rst 45 | est 15 | page 83
>
> [Read the following.]

Co-parenting requires the parents to work together while actively making individual contributions for the benefit of the children. Co-parenting in a family is critical to the success of the children and family, even when the parents do not live together.

5.2.a Family Sculpturing

> **Note:** For this exercise, provide three chairs in the front of the room. The best type of chairs to use are stackable. Remember to show appreciation and encouragement for those who volunteer.
>
> **Instruct:** *We are going to do a family sculpture using three chairs. Volunteers will have an opportunity to arrange the chairs in a way to represent a healthy family. They will arrange the chairs, identify which chair represents the father, mother, and child, and then say how the arrangement highlights a healthy family.*

Instructions: We are going to do a family sculpture using three chairs. Volunteers will have an opportunity to arrange the chairs in a way to represent a healthy family. They will arrange the chairs, identify which chair represents the father, mother, and child, and then say how the arrangement highlights a healthy family.

> **Note:** You will share the final arrangement representing a healthy family.
>
> [Place two chairs side by side. Stack the third chair on top of the two chairs.]
>
> **State:** *The arrangement shows the father and mother connected in a lifelong relationship as the foundation of the family. Together they lovingly support the child. The child can learn from models of how a man treats a woman and a woman treats a man. The child is not in the middle of the relationship.*
>
> **Summary:** *This exercise suggests the benefit of the family on the child. Both the father and mother are critical to the child. It is better when the child has access to the unique contributions of the mother and father.*

5.2.b Getting Past the Drama

> **State:** *Cooperation is the key to getting past the drama.*
>
> [Read the following.]

What do you work towards when you have a family? You should COOPERATE, meaning that you both try to find an answer or solution that works for both of you. These are the steps for cooperating:

1. Take turns talking and listening
2. Offer trades
3. Stop and calm down if you are angry

Problem Solving

After you have scheduled a time for everyone involved to get together and work on solving the problem, it is a good idea to make a plan. The following steps can help make the process easier:

1. *State the Problem.*
2. *Write or Discuss the Results You Want.* Be sure to be as specific as possible.
3. *List All Possible Solutions.* Listen to everyone's ideas, and do not dismiss anyone's idea as stupid or impossible.
4. *Review the List Together.* Go over the list with everyone needed to solve the problem.
5. *Each Person Should Choose Two Solutions They Are Willing to Carry Out.*
6. *Decide on a Solution.*
7. *Decide on an Action Plan.* After your group has decided on a solution, decide what tasks need to be done and who will carry them out. Plan to meet to evaluate the progress of the solution.

5.2.c Co-parenting Tips

> **State:** *Following are some practical co-parenting tips that can make cooperating easier.*
>
> [Read the following.]

1. Respect the child's mother and practice treating her like you want to be treated.
2. Practice trying to see things from your child and your child's mother's point of view.
3. Communicate directly and never through the children.
4. Share information with your partner.
5. Support your co-parent's role with your child and to your child.
6. Recognize the boundary of her home, be careful with advice, and don't criticize.
7. Refresh and work on yourself when you don't have your child(ren).

Instructions: From this section describe what you can work on to improve your co-parenting, whether or not you live with your child's mother.

_____

_____

_____

_____

_____

5.3 Better Dad Skills

> rct 90 | rst 30 | est 15 | page 85
>
> **State:** *There are three simple dad skills that can strengthen your effectiveness as a father. These skills are investing your time, leading and role-modeling, and caring for your child.*
>
> **State:** *Next, we will take a closer look at each skill.*
>
> [Read/Summarize the following.]

5.3.a Investing Your Time

What does a healthy father look like? There are three important aspects of important fathering skills:

1. The father (and mother) is in charge of the family
2. The father gives everyone room, including self, to be close and apart
3. The father is flexible when it comes to change

The two important roles of the father are to lead and model. To be successful in life, children need to learn to feel good about themselves and to get along with other people. The father needs to commit to help the child develop a positive sense of himself/herself and develop the ability to make and keep friends. One of the ways that the father acts as a leader is by making rules for the family.

5.3.b Leading and Role Modeling

Rules without relationship leads to rebellion. Here are three guides for making rules:

1. Make rules for what you want, not don't want
2. Make rules with results you can see or measure
3. State the rule in a sentence and be specific

You and your families have been through many changes. Changes occur as people get older, move into their own apartments, marry, find new jobs, have children, and die. Change can be exciting, but it can also be difficult. The following are some general rules for change:

1. **Expect Change.** Remember that changes are normal. All families go through change—some ordinary and some not so ordinary.
2. **Stress Is a Signal that Change Is Necessary.** Do you know how to tell when you are feeling stress? It could be that you feel worried or upset, or you could be angry or sick. When you are feeling like this, it probably means that you need to make a change in some area of your life, maybe find a new way of doing something.
3. **Expect to Feel Resistance in Others and Yourself.** Change is hard. People usually try to continue without making any changes for as long as possible. Just remember that change is normal, and it is also normal to not want to change. Hopefully, this will help reduce the amount of time you spend fighting change.
4. **Take One Step at a Time.** Change takes time. It is easier to deal with if you are able to focus on one small step at a time.
5. **Ask Someone for Help if You Are Stuck.** Family, friends, teachers, and religious leaders are all good sources of help.
6. **Anticipate Areas Where Children Will Need a Rule and Make It.** e.g., "When the guests arrive, the television is to be turned off."
7. **Get Your Children's Thoughts on Rules that Affect Them.** This is especially true as they get older. Then, you make the final decision. E.g., "You want to drive the car to a dance and we're worried about your showing off or getting in an accident Tell us why you think you are ready for it."
8. **Only Make Rules You Are Prepared to Enforce.**
9. **Consider Your Own Comfort,** as well as your child's needs in deciding on rules. (e.g., "You would like to stay up until 10 p.m., but your mother and I need some time to ourselves. Bedtime is 9 p.m.")
10. **Expect Resistance.** Feel free to change any rule you made which no longer gets the result you want. E.g., "Now that summer is here, it's ok to get home by 6 p.m. instead of 4 p.m."

Family Meeting

A good way for families to solve problems and to know what is going on with each other is to have a family meeting. The following things should happen in a family meeting:

- Have one meeting per week.
- The meeting should last one hour at the most.
- Only one person should speak at a time.
- Making fun of each other and name-calling cannot happen.
- Everyone will have a turn to speak.
- Everyone should say one thing that is going right.
- Any problems should be identified.
- Pick one problem to solve.
- Stay focused on what people want and how to get it, not on complaints
- Plan a fun activity for next week.

Our group can also have "family meetings" to help us make decisions, plan activities, and solve problems. In our first meeting, we will work together to decide what kind of rules we want to make for participation in our group. Let's try to make rules for what we want, not for what we don't want. We also need to decide on consequences, both good and bad.

5.3.c Caring for Your Child

State: *In the movie* John Q, *during the first 15 minutes of the movie you see a family that is full of nurturing. We see them waking up together to hardship, but working through it together. They eat, ride to school, go to church, and their sons game together. Next, we will do a "word find" of nurturing behaviors from the movie.*

[Read the instructions and do the exercise.]

Instructions: Find the words below that describe nurturing.

Nurture Word Find

A	F	N	S	H	R	E	T	A	M	L	Y
O	C	I	U	S	R	T	S	N	O	A	H
K	G	M	S	T	E	E	I	A	L	C	P
P	A	U	A	T	V	A	F	P	R	T	I
M	L	D	H	O	B	E	N	U	V	C	H
Z	A	E	L	N	E	U	H	H	Q	E	S
E	R	K	F	S	B	C	M	S	B	L	D
P	U	X	E	I	S	T	D	P	U	A	N
J	T	B	L	U	R	S	F	P	L	U	I
R	O	W	J	L	P	N	I	Y	A	G	E
A	N	K	D	F	H	O	N	K	B	H	R
V	O	T	E	R	A	C	N	A	N	I	F

Word Bank: Hug, Kiss, Fist Bump, Make up, Love, Care, Joke, Laugh, Play.

Be affectionate, especially as they get older. Kids need love, but not just words alone.

Kids do understand a loving touch. Hugging them, snuggling them, and kissing them makes them feel loved. It's a basic way humans communicate love, but some fathers feel awkward showing love in this way. Get over it. A kid needs to feel loved, always, and you have within your power a guaranteed way to make them know they're loved. A kid that knows they're loved is a happy kid—the kind of kid that runs and jumps into your arms when they see you.

You will never, never regret being affectionate with your child, because you will be able to send a "you're loved" message right to your kid's heart anytime with just a simple peck on the forehead, a quick hug before school, or even just tousling their hair as they walk by. A dad's loving touch is amazingly powerful; it sends a message to your child that words can't always convey. By the way, high-fiving doesn't count. It's a celebration—not a sign of affection.

Treat your kid the way you wanted to be treated when you were a kid. Take a look back on how you were raised. Look back at how your dad showed, or didn't show, his love for you—how he disciplined you, encouraged you, criticized you, and molded you. If you had a great dad, now is your chance to take everything he showed you and put it to good use.

If you didn't have a great dad, this is your chance, your golden opportunity to make up for every fatherly injustice he did to you by being to your child a much better and more sensitive, involved, loving dad than he was to you. This is your chance to show your dad, and the world, "This is what being a good dad looks like." Provide your child with a level of love, patience, understanding, and affection that shows your own dad how it's done.

Don't ever abuse your kid. Ever. The same goes for your wife. There is never, ever a reason to hit a woman or abuse a child. It is the height of cowardice and a disgrace to fathers everywhere to hurt any woman or child. It is impossible to be a great dad if you hurt your child or your child's mommy even once. It dishonors you, your entire life, and everything you've worked this hard to achieve. Pass this on to your kids.

Besides hitting, never be verbally cruel to your child. Never call him stupid, an idiot, or any name that makes him think he's less than the special child he is. Make it your goal to give your kid so much love and praise that it gives him a high self-esteem problem.

5.4 The Dad Plan

> rct 75 | rst 15 | est 15 | page 90
>
> **State:** *This section is one of the most important parts of the course, where you put knowledge into action.*
>
> **Instruct:** *Answer the following questions to create your Dad Plan to improve your relational and co-parenting skills.*

Fathering Skill: Become a better dad by improving my relational skills, my co-parenting, and my role as a father.

Remember to use SMART goals for your plan to turn your life around.

Instructions: Answer the following questions to create your Dad Plan to become a better dad.

1. What is my specific SMART (Specific, Measurable, Achievable, Realistic, Timetable) goal for growing in cultural awareness?
2. What can I do every day this week to grow more culturally aware?
3. When and where will I do this?
4. Who will hold me accountable?

6.0 Moving Forward

rct 60 | rst 60 | est 15 | page 91

[Read the following.]

GOAL

To become a better dad,
no matter how tough, I won't quit or give up,
through the support of my faith, family, and community,
until my last breath and my eyes finally shut.

OBJECTIVES

1. Child support
2. Employment
3. Overcoming addiction

6.1 Child Support

> **State:** *What value or price would you place on your child? To most parents, their child is worth everything. Child support is intended for the child and is a minimum amount paid by the non-custodial parent that contributes to the financial needs of the child.*
>
> **State:** *Next, we will do an exercise to start the discussion on child support.*
>
> **Instruct:** *The facilitator will instruct the class on making a Dart paper airplane. Once the Dart has been constructed, you will have an opportunity for a couple of practice flights.*
>
> [Give participants a one-minute warning when the time is up.]

6.1.a Activity: Aircraft Carrier Support

Instructions: The facilitator will instruct the class on making a Dart paper airplane. Once the Dart has been constructed, you will have an opportunity for a couple of practice flights.

The Dart is a "jet" and a designated table will be an "aircraft carrier." The objective is throwing your Dart in such a way as to land it on the table. Once all Darts have been completed we will take turns to attempt to land the plane on an aircraft carrier (table).

> [Ask the process questions.]

Process Questions

1. How does an aircraft carrier support the aircraft?
2. What is child support?
3. How much support should you give your child?
4. What are other ways you support your child?
5. Can you think of a situation where you would not support your child?

1.0 Child support is intended to be a minimum amount paid by the non-custodial parent to contribute to the financial needs of the child.

6.1.b How DADS Can Help

> **State:** *The child support system at times may feel like a hostile adversary of fathers. During those times, the system seems to communicate a message to the dads that their only purpose is to pay or die.*
>
> **State:** *The majority of men (at least 51% and, of course, the percentage is higher) want to support their children.*
>
> [Read the following and instruct on the activity].

There is no worse description of single fathers who have gone underground than the label "deadbeat dad." This is a terribly unjust condemnation to put upon a man who finds himself in the no-win situation of being damned if he does (seeking legitimate work and paying what the system says he owes for child support) and damned if he doesn't (going off the radar, doing "under the table" day labor jobs, or engaging in criminal behavior). It is not as simple as it may sound; the situations are more often complex.

Instruction: List three factors that get in the way of men paying child support.

1. _____

2. _____

3. _____

Process Question: How can we get past these barriers?

Next, we will review the five steps to "Becoming Dads" who are striving to be better.

1. **Face the Reality**—The first step is an honest look at our current situation of housing, transportation, legal issues, addiction, family violence, income, and employment, and consider how we all can be more involved with our child(ren).
2. **Turn Around**—The second step is making a decision to change your situation, to repent or stop going the way you've been going and going another way. Be willing to take the time and make the effort to make the changes to become the dad your child needs.
3. **My Dad Plan**—Make a plan to become a safe person for your child, recover from addiction and family violence, to give your child a place to stay in a home, transportation to get where your child needs to go, a father who is not in danger of incarceration, a father who can provide for the needs of his child, and a father who has time for his child.
4. **The Parenting Plan**—A parenting plan or custody plan outlines how you and the other parent will continue to care and provide for your children after you separate. An effective plan contains a parenting time schedule that shows when your child is with each parent and how the exchange is made, who has legal custody and the authority to make decisions about the child, medical and health care information that explain how the parent pays for medical and dental costs and who provides medical insurance, where your child will attend school and who pays and engages at the school, what are the guidelines to follow in raising your child, and how the parents will communicate and work together.
5. **Work with DADS**—Divine Alternatives for Dads Services is here to come alongside of you. We will help you understand and work with the system, show how faith can help you turn your situation around, help you take practical steps to improve your situation, and be your fan who will believe in you and encourage you with hope that life can be different for you and your child.

6.1 The majority of men want to support their child and DADS can help.

6.1.c Frequently Asked Questions

> **State:** *In this section, we will review some of the frequently asked questions about child support. We are not going to cover everything in this section, but it will serve as a reference for you.*
>
> [Highlight the following sections that you think might be useful for the men.]

Child support is a topic that tends to polarize all parties involved. Although in some situations mothers pay child support to custodial fathers, in the vast majority of cases, mothers are the custodial parents and non-custodial fathers pay child support. So, how does the child support system work, and what does a father need to know in order to manage his obligations?

The State Program for Parents

DADS was the model for the Alternative Solutions Program, a statewide initiative within the Division of Child Support (DCS) aimed at helping parents toward self-sufficiency. DCS puts great value on the non-custodial parent's role in their communities and with their families. While most parents pay their child support, others have trouble meeting their responsibility. DADS' well-rounded approach to child support services works as a bridge between community groups and the people they help, dealing with issues such as joblessness, housing, medical, legal issues, and transition from jail and prison.

The Alternative Solutions Program links parents with government and community groups to increase their ability to get a job and be financially stable. When you take part in the Alternative Solutions Program, your case worker will work with you to create an action plan for you that could:

- Work with local partners that can help with finding a job, training, housing, food, and medical and legal resources
- Help lower your monthly DCS payments or state-owed debt
- Help with license suspension and other case actions

With a database of over 3,500 community resources in the state, we can connect you to the services you need.

How Long Child Support Lasts

Generally, the law requires a person paying child support to make those payments until (1) your child is no longer a minor, unless the child has special needs, (2) the child becomes active-duty military, (3) your parental rights are terminated through adoption or another legal process, or (4) your minor child is declared "emancipated" by a court—that is, declared an adult earlier than normal because of the ability to be self-supporting.

How a Custody Decision Impacts Child Support

Both parents have a responsibility to support their children financially. When a divorce occurs and one parent has physical custody of the children, that parent's responsibility is fulfilled by being the custodial parent. The other parent then makes a child support payment which fulfills that non-custodial parent's financial responsibilities. In the case of joint custody, the amount of child support each pays is normally calculated by the court considering the percentage each parent contributes to the couple's joint income and the percentage of time each parent has physical custody of the children.

Child Support Responsibilities When Not Married

The obligation to support a child is not conditioned by marriage. If you are a parent, you have a responsibility to financially support your offspring. Your parental responsibilities can be legally determined either through your acknowledgment that you are a parent, by the fact that you had welcomed the child into your home as your own, or as established by a paternity test.

State laws vary somewhat on the definition of a parent, so if there is some doubt about your parentage, you will want to consult with a family law attorney in your state.

It also happens at times that a man who fathered a child may not be asked to pay child support until the child's mother receives public assistance. In that case, the government may come to the father seeking back child support to reimburse the government for its assistance payments. Many fathers have been "blindsided" by these orders many years after the fact.

Stepfather's Financial Liability

If a stepfather legally adopts the children and thus terminates the parental rights of the biological father, the stepfather becomes liable for their financial support.

How the Amount of Child Support Is Determined

Each state in the United States is required by federal law to establish guidelines used to calculate child support due from parents based largely on their income and expenses. Because states have a fair amount of discretion in setting these guidelines, child support payments required vary widely between states, even under the same circumstances. But, normally, the courts will take into account issues like the standard of living of the child prior to divorce, the specific needs of the child, the resources of the custodial parent, and the non-custodial parent's ability to pay. Because in most states judges are allowed wide discretion in setting these payments, it is important for a non-custodial father to get as much information on the table with the court up-front to make the payments as fair as possible.

How Earnings Change Impacts Calculations If Underemployed or Returning to School

This depends on the judge and the circumstances. But, generally, a child support payment would not be reduced if a father quit a full-time job and returned to school. If he became unemployed and then took a lower paying job, a reconsideration of the amount of child support due might be appropriate.

Consequences of Not Making Child Support Payments as Ordered

Not staying current on your child support obligations is called "big trouble." You are inviting a lot of legal involvement in your life and finances if you don't live up to your mandated child support obligations. Additionally, it can hurt your credibility with the court and with state enforcement officials if you want to later make changes to your parenting plan, your custody arrangements, or other aspects of the legal relationship with your kids and your former spouse.

The court order entered as a part of your divorce and custody process defines the amount and payment schedule, as well as other conditions that might lead to recalibrating your commitments. These conditions might prescribe how much of a new raise might be added to your support obligations, or what you can do with a windfall such as an inheritance or an insurance settlement.

Failing to meet the schedule is seen as defying an order of the court and could land you in jail, resulting in a garnishment of your wages, intercepting your tax refund, seizing property, suspending your business license or driver's license, or other serious consequences.

Garnishment is sometimes the most difficult as it involves your employer holding back some, most, or all of your income and remitting it to the state. When paying your back obligations involves your employer, it could create some unintended negative consequences at work.

While Title III of the federal Consumer Credit Protection Act prohibits an employer from firing an employee for having a garnishment for any single indebtedness, you could be in trouble with your employer for multiple garnishments. Others that could come beyond your child support garnishments (like back taxes or other debts) could result in your being fired. So this is clearly something you want to avoid at almost any cost.

If you are having difficulty meeting your child support obligations, you might consider creating a more realistic budget, reducing your expenses, finding less expensive housing, getting a cheaper car, or negotiating with creditors to lower your monthly debt obligation payments. These may seem like drastic measures and may really change your life, but a more austere lifestyle may be necessary in order that you can meet your obligations and provide for the care of your children.

If you become unemployed, take a pay cut, have large medical bills, or have some other extenuating circumstance, it is important that you begin the process immediately to have your child support amount modified.

You would start by contacting your state's child support enforcement office and requesting to file a formal motion to modify your child support obligations. It is in your best interest to start this process as soon as something significant changes. In most cases, the law prohibits a judge from retroactively reducing a child support payment, even if a reduction is reasonable after the fact. And, you will remain on the hook for the amounts required before the effective date of the modified child support order.

Getting behind on your child support payments is something you need to think seriously about. Neglecting this important responsibility can have far-reaching consequences and is a lot more critical than many other choices you can make when times get tough financially. Just go in with your eyes wide open.

Your Options If Child(ren)'s Mother Refuses to Pay Court-Ordered Support

Federal law requires the state or district attorney to help you collect delinquent child support payments. Most states have an entire bureaucracy—usually called something like the Office of Recovery Services—available to collect these payments, and you should start there.

If Your Circumstances Have Changed

Only the court can change a mandated child support payment, so any modification would have to be submitted to a judge. If both spouses agree on a change, it is usually a pretty simple process. When you don't agree, the request will be submitted by your family law attorney for a hearing. The spouse who wants to make a change over the other's objection has the burden to show what has changed and why a different amount (higher or lower) should be required. Temporary changes might be the result of a medical emergency, a change in employment status, or a short-term economic hardship on the part of the receiving parent.

A permanent change in child support is often considered when income changes due to a remarriage, either parent has a job change that affects ability to pay, or the child involved has new and different needs than were contemplated when the original amount was set.

Withholding Child Support If Your Ex Doesn't Honor Custody or Visitation Orders

This is one of the biggest complaints of non-custodial fathers. Unfortunately, this is not permissible. Child support payments and visitation are considered by the law to be totally separate issues. If your ex is not living up to the custody decree by providing visitation as required, you will need to go back to court to enforce the court order. You have an obligation to financially support your children, regardless of any visitation issues.

6.2 Employment

> rct 45 | rst 45 | est 15 | page 98
>
> **State:** *Our own needs and the needs of the children that depend on us require income, which requires employment. Not only do we need employment but employment that provides a livable wage that can provide the income to meet all our obligations.*
>
> **State:** *There are many paths to employment, which include education, special training, starting your own business, or working for someone else. In this section, we will explore important conditions in finding desirable employment.*
>
> [Read the following.

Employment is a necessity to meet our needs and the needs of our child. There are many paths to employment, which include education, special training, starting your own business, or working for someone else. In this section, we will explore important conditions of finding desirable employment.

6.2.a Activity: 30-Second Commercial

> **State:** *If you had 30 seconds to introduce yourself to a possible employer, what would you say? In this section, we will do an activity that can help you obtain any job you for which you will ever be hired.*
>
> [Read the following and instruct on the 30-Second Commercial (3SC).]

A "30-second commercial" (3SC) could be your best chance to make a good impression on a potential employer. And just like a television advertiser who is trying to sell a product will spend time and money getting it just right, you can spend time and practice to get it just right so you can be hired.

What does a 3SC contain? Here is an outline of the 3SC:

1. **Greeting:** (Pleasant smile, firm handshake, speak clearly) "I am pleased to meet you. My name is (your first and last name)."
2. **Education, Experience, and Skills:** (Where did you go to school, what did you study, who did you work for, what did you do, any special skills)
3. **Strengths:** (Character qualities like "hard-working," "creative," or "good communicator")
4. **Accomplishments:** (Recognition, awards, or accomplishments that highlight your strengths and achievements)
5. **Goal:** (What kind of job/career are you looking for?)

Instructions: Make a list of items for each category and then use these items to create your 30-second commercial.

Greeting	1.
Education, Experience, and Skills	1. 2. 3.
Strengths	1. 2. 3.
Accomplishments	1. 2. 3.
Goal	1.

6.2.b Soft Skills

State: *What are soft skills? They are characteristics that enable someone to work effectively together with other people. Soft skills are those things that help a person to be a good team player.*

Instruct: *In the diagram below, label the outline of the man with your top five characteristics of a team player (having important soft skills).*

Instructions: In the diagram below, label the outline of the man with your top five characteristics of being a team player (having important soft skills).

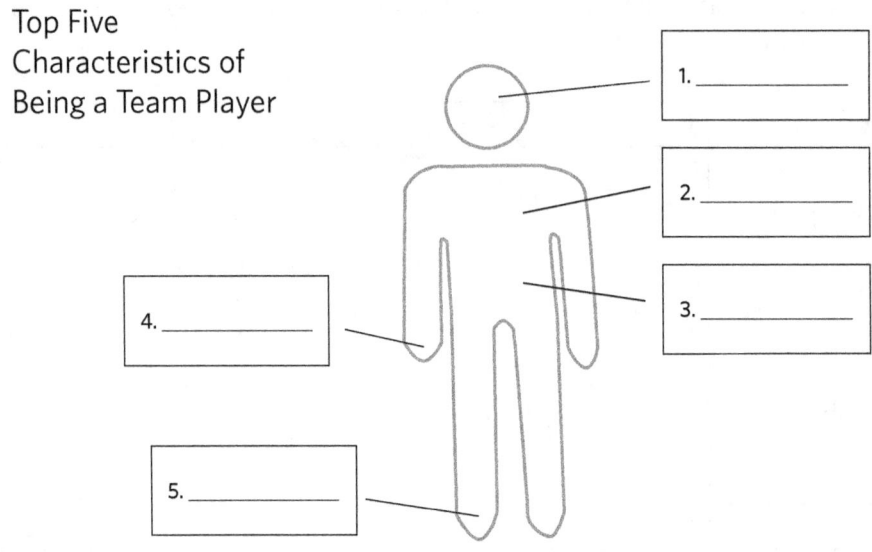

Top Five Characteristics of Being a Team Player

1. _____
2. _____
3. _____
4. _____
5. _____

[Give men the time to complete the activity and then review their responses; be sure to encourage them.]

State: *Next, we will review what companies say they are looking for in soft skills. You may have listed the same qualities.*

[Review the lists.]

A Positive Attitude

Employers seek employees who take the initiative and have the motivation to get the job done in a reasonable period of time. A positive attitude gets the work done and motivates others to do the same without dwelling on the challenges that inevitably come up in any job.

It is the enthusiastic employee who creates an environment of good will and who provides a positive role model for others. A positive attitude is something that is most valued by supervisors and co-workers, and that also makes the job more pleasant and fun to go to each day.

A Good Work Ethic

A strong work ethic is something a potential employer will want to see. A strong work ethic can be demonstrated by your ability to follow through on your duties and responsibilities and always ensure the work is done completely and according to procedures. Commitment is another characteristic that goes along with a strong work ethic. Be at work on time, do what you were hired to do, meet targets and deadlines, and work to the best of your ability. What more could an employer ask?

Excellent Communication Skills

This includes the ability to communicate clearly and effectively in many mediums: by email, verbally, with lists and phone messages, on the phone, and with body language. Communication also includes listening skills and the ability to follow directions and provide feedback.

Problem Solving

Companies are looking for people who are motivated to take on challenges with minimal direction. Employees should see when something needs to be done and react accordingly.

A Team Player

Employers and managers like to have people working with them and for them who can get along with their colleagues, and who can work with others effectively in different circumstances.

Leadership

Do you see this individual being a significant part of your company and leading future employees of the firm? Leadership begins with self-confidence, and is molded by positive reinforcement and repetitive success.

Innovative Thinking

Companies always need creative team members to help find new solutions. One of the benefits of new hires is new ideas, but to make sure you get new ideas you need creative thinkers.

6.2.c Preparing for Employment

> **State:** *Filling out an application is your lasting presentation of yourself to the potential employer. An application is like a resume that represents you. There are two reasons this is important. The first is that it can help you get the job and the second is it can give you a good picture of what you need to do to make your application stronger.*
>
> [Review the aspects of the application process.]

Picking it up: When you pick up or drop off an application, be prepared for an interview. You never know if they will have a few minutes and are in a hurry to hire someone. Also, dress appropriately because, even though you may not get an interview that day, the secretary or person who takes the application may be asked by the interviewer what they thought of you. First impressions are important; you only get one time to make one, so you want to make it good.

Read carefully: Read the entire form carefully. Know what is being asked before filling out the form. Employers may use the application form to judge how well you follow instructions and how careful you may be as an employee. Fill in the blanks and answer all questions. Fill in the blanks completely, accurately, and truthfully. When something doesn't apply to you, write N/A for "non-applicable." Check your answers for correct spelling, grammar, punctuation, completeness, and accuracy.

Ink/Type: Use blue or black ink or type the application (no funky colors!). Print clearly. Position: Avoid the word "anything." Put a specific job down to show you're not desperate and that you have a goal in mind.

Salary expected: Employers may use this question to screen out applicants. It is best to give a salary range or to respond with "negotiable." Use one of these responses even if you know the wage. This leaves you room to negotiate a higher wage.

Personal information: If you don't have a phone, give a number where messages can be left for you.

Education and training: List academic, vocational, and professional education and schools attended. Be prepared to attach copies of certificates or other documents. If you are planning to attend college, write "Plan to attend XYZ College" and when.

Work experience: Always list the most recent employer first. Give complete and accurate names, dates, addresses, phone numbers, job titles, dates of employment, etc. Use your resume as a guide. Make sure the information presented in the application agrees with the information in your resume. Explain gaps in your work history.

Special job-related skills: Use action verbs to list your special job-related skills, training, licenses, and accomplishments. List the types of equipment/tools that you can use. This will make you stand out from other applicants. The job description can provide clues about important skills.

Reason for leaving: Be careful when giving your reason for leaving a previous job. Even if your previous boss was a jerk, you should never be negative. Acceptable answers include: "school conflict," "conflicting hours," "better opportunities for advancement," "lack of work," or "seasonal employment."

References: Most employers will call references, but they also may request a written evaluation by mail. Many employers can only tell dates worked and if they would re-hire you. Therefore, you may want to use teachers, counselors, principals, coaches, ministers, etc. as references. (Do not use relatives.) Be sure to ask for their permission and verify where they can be reached. Provide complete and accurate information about three (or more) people who can speak highly of you.

Last details: Sign (don't print) your name and include the current date. Check carefully that you have completed the application. Once you fill out an application, it is a binding document; any misinformation could be grounds for termination. If you are asked when you can begin work, be sure to allow enough time to give at least two weeks' notice to your current employer.

Instruct: *Filling out the application.*

[Review the aspects of the application process.]

Instructions: Fill out the application.

Personal Information
Name, Address, Phone

Position Applying For

Desired Wage

Have you ever been convicted of felony?

Employment History (Last three jobs)

Education

[   ]

Special Skills

[   ]

References

[   ]

6.2 We need employment that provides a livable wage to meet all our personal obligations, including meeting the needs of our children.

6.3 Addictions

> rct 30 | rst 30 | est 15 | page 105
>
> **State:** *Addiction is like a tornado. It is often not seen coming until it is too late. It tears through your life and the lives of people you know. In its wake, it leaves a path of destruction on everything it touches. Once caught in the addiction tornado, your life can spin into a cycle of drugs, crime, and incarceration. Addiction is a matter of life and death.*
>
> **State:** *However, there is hope; many people have found a path to recovery. In this section, we seek to better understand addiction and how we can get on the path to recovery.*

Addiction is like a tornado. It is often not seen coming until it is too late. It tears through your life and the lives of people you know. In its wake, it leaves of path of destruction on everything it touches. Once caught in the addiction tornado, your life can spin in a cycle of drugs, crime, and incarceration. Addiction is a matter of life and death.

However, there is hope, many people have found a path to recovery. In this section, we seek to better understand addiction and how we can get on the path to recovery.

6.3 Activity: Paper Football Game

> [Read the instructions, perform the activity, and discuss the process questions.]

Instructions: The facilitator will instruct you on making a simple football and explaining the rules. We will pair up and play a four-minute game of paper football.

1. Move the ball by flicking with thumb and forefinger.
2. A touchdown is scored when a player advances the ball so that part of it is extended over the edge of the table. Player also gets a "kick" for an extra point.
3. A kick is scored when the ball is held by one hand and flicked with the other hand, and travels through the goalpost formed by the finger of the opposing team.
4. If the opponent flicks the ball off the table four times, the opposing player gets to kick a field goal.

Process Questions

1. How would you define addiction?
2. How would you compare this game to addiction?
3. What are some things that may help you win?
4. What are some things that may cause you to lose?

6.3a Substance Use Disorder

> **Note:** The purpose of this section is to give the participants a better understanding of Substance Use Disorder to help with recovery.
>
> [Read the following.]

Many people simply do not understand how a person can have a predisposition to addiction or develop a substance use disorder. They attribute substance use disorder to a breakdown of moral character, lack of willpower, or foolishness, and assume the user could easily stop at any time. The reality is that Substance Use Disorder is complex, and it takes more than good intentions and a strong will to recover.

The initial decision to use drugs is voluntary for most people, but repeated use is what often leads to brain changes that challenge the user's self-control and interfere with their ability to resist the urge to use. Because of these changes, the user is highly susceptible to relapsing even after years of sobriety (Gould, 2010; Volkow et al., 2004).

> **State:** *When does substance use become a disorder? Next, we will look at the symptoms of SUD.*
>
> [Read the following; lead the exercise.]
> [Answer key:
> Impairment control—4th box
> Social impairment—3rd box
> Risky use—2nd box
> Pharmacological criteria—1st box]

SUD Symptoms

Substance Use Disorder represents a cluster of symptoms that indicate the individual continues using the substance despite the resulting related problems of various degrees of severity. The pathological patterns of behaviors related to the use of all substances can be grouped into four areas: impairment control, social impairment, risky use, and pharmacological criteria.

Instructions: Match the patterns of behavior of Substance Use Disorder with the descriptions of the behavior by drawing a line connecting the words on the left with a box on the right.

1. Impairment control	a. A tolerance requires markedly higher doses to achieve the same desired result. b. After prolonged use, a sudden cessation can result in a variety of withdrawal symptoms.
2. Social impairment	a. Substances used in situations that are physically hazardous. b. Continued used despite knowledge of having problems that is made worse by the substance. c. Failure to abstain despite the difficulty it causes.
3. Risky Use	a. Failure in obligations at work, school, and home. b. Continued use despite persistent or recurrent social problems due to the effects of substance. c. Important social, work, or recreational activities may be given up or reduced due to usage. d. May withdraw from family and hobbies in order to use substances.
4. Pharmacological criteria	a. Take the substance in larger amounts or over a longer period than intended. b. Express a persistent desire to cut down or regulate the substance and report repeated unsuccessful efforts to cut down or stop. c. Spend large amounts of time searching, using, and recovering from the substance. d. Almost all daily activities revolve around the substance. e. Overwhelming craving may occur at any time but likely triggered by a conditioned association with some type of internal or external trigger.

> **State:** *Next, we will look at five factors that can influence SUD.*
>
> [Read the following; lead the exercise.]
> Answer key:
> 1. Attachment
> 2. Trauma
> 3. Biology
> 4. Environment
> 5. Cognition

SUD Factors

There is no single factor that can predict whether a person will have a SUD. However, there are five factors that can influence Substance Use Disorder (see figure 6.3).

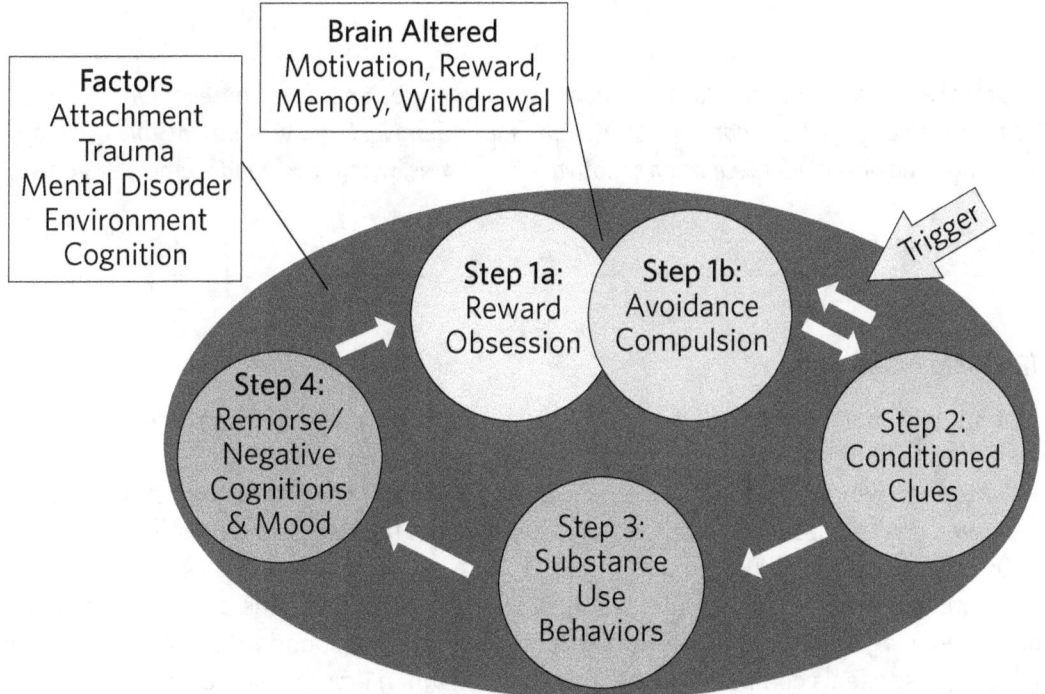

Instructions: Using the Word Bank below fill in the blanks.
Word Bank: (Environment, Biology, Trauma, Cognition, Attachment)

1. Having an insecure _____ caused by a mother or caregiver that was not responsive and reliable in meeting your needs in the first three months of your life. This makes gaining and maintaining social support difficult.
2. Experiencing _____ which is not resolved can result in repeated reliving of the experience and seeking relief of the symptoms through substance use.
3. _____ accounts for about half a person's risk for addiction. Having a biological parent with Alcohol Use Disorder increases the likelihood of developing the disorder, even if adopted into a family with no alcohol use disorder.
4. A person's _____ is a factor; for example, certain groups are prone to Alcohol Use Disorders, including males, people with low education and income, people who have divorced, and people in certain occupations with a drinking culture.
5. Our _____ drives the thousands of words we say to ourselves daily; this is called self-talk. Most of our self-talk is negative, which can lead to the negative behaviors of substance use.

> **State:** *We just examined five factors that can influence substance use. These factors are part of the cycle of addiction that is illustrated in Figure 6.3. Next, we will look at this cycle of addiction and how it alters our brain's motivation, rewards, withdrawal, and memory systems.*
>
> [Read the following.

The Cycle of Addiction

Most drugs stimulate a flood of the brain's chemical messenger dopamine, a reward center (see figure 6.3 Step1a). This reward center controls the body's ability to feel pleasure and motivates behaviors needed to thrive (e.g., eating and socializing). This overstimulation of the reward center causes the intensely pleasurable high that leads to repeated use (Gould, 2010; Volkow et al., 2004).

Continued use causes the brain to adjust to the excess dopamine by making less of it and/or reducing the ability of cells in the reward center to respond to it. This reduces the high the person feels compared to the high they felt when first taking the drug—i.e., tolerance. The reaction is taking more to obtain the same high. Additionally, it may cause less pleasure from other things previously enjoyed, like eating or social activities (Gould, 2010; Volkow et al., 2004). In other words, the user requires the substance just to feel normal and avoid feeling bad (see Figure 6.3 Step 1b).

Other cues from the environment (senses, memories, places, feelings, etc.) that are associated with the high (see figure 6.3 Step 2) can trigger the craving to seek the substance, use the substance (see figure 6.3 Step 3), experience the remorse of using (see figure 6.3 Step 4), and repeat the cycle.

Process Questions:

1. How do you know if you have a substance use disorder?
2. What factors in your own life make you susceptible to addiction?
3. What makes the addiction cycle so difficult to break?

6.3 A combination of biology, environment, and developmental factors influence the risk for substance use disorder.

6.3b Preparing to Change

> **State:** *Next, we will look at how we make changes and some of the preparations we need to make in order to change.*
>
> [Read the instructions and facilitate the exercise, and review the preparation for change.]

As covered in the first session, there are five stages people cycle through several times before they actually make a change (Prochaska, DiClemente and Norcross, 1992). The stages are: maintenance, preparation, relapse, pre-contemplation, action, and contemplation.

1. Pre-contemplation: You do not see a need to change right now.
2. Contemplation: You see a need for change and are thinking about changing.
3. Preparation: You intend to take action in the near future.
4. Action: You change your behavior.
5. Maintenance: You need to sustain the change and not slip back into the rut.
6. Relapse: You begin again.

Change is not easy, and after you change, you can often fall back into old patterns, so you have to keep trying.

We Are Resistant to Change

The concept of homeostasis is from the field of biology. The human body regulates itself to keep a steady state of homeostasis (Cannon, 1932). An example is that when our body temperature gets above 98.6, it perspires to cool the body back to equilibrium. In short, any change in the body is met with resistance, and an attempt is made to change it back.

This concept is also used in family therapy. The idea is that families and individuals resist change to maintain the steady state. This is what keeps families and individuals stuck in cycles or behaviors. It is like a car getting stuck in a rut. The car wheel is trying to roll forward, but cannot get the momentum to break free and rolls right back into the rut.

Recognizing Our Discrepancy

People are more persuaded by what they hear themselves say than by what other people tell them. Helping the family focus attention on how current behavior differs from ideal or desired behavior is an important step in making a change. An example is, your goal or desire is to be a happy family together, but your substance use is causing the family pain and tearing it apart.

This requires listening to what the family expresses as their goals or values. You can help change the family's perception without creating a sense of being pressured or coerced. The change in the family is motivated by the perceived discrepancy between current family functioning and important family goals and values.

Finding a Support Group

Families and friends who've been affected by addiction also need comfort and support. By associating with other family members who are going through a similar situation, it helps them advance in their own recovery process. This is how emotional healing begins, and why support groups for families of drug addicts are so important.

Support groups allow members to help each other. Many of us learn the most when we teach others. For those who devote their time and energy to helping others in recovery, the emotional and psychological benefits are quite tangible. By not only receiving support, but by also giving it, a member's involvement is increased, and more is gained from the experience.

While support groups for drug and alcohol abuse aren't the final answers to recovery's questions, they're extremely beneficial to the process. Those who participate in these groups generally have a more positive attitude towards their treatment and are better equipped to maintain sustained recovery.

Process Questions:
1. Why is change so difficult?
2. How does the stages of change model help you think about successful change?

6.3b We are resistant to change, but by recognizing how our substance use keeps us from our deepest desires or goals and through the support of others, we can change.

6.3c Step Up to Change

> **State:** *Often stepping up to change requires the help of others, such as with the success that has been shown through Motivational Interviewing and 12 Steps.*
>
> [Review the following.]

Motivational Interviewing (MI) is a counseling style that was initially used to treat addiction but is increasingly being used for other social-helping professions. MI can be used to create an environment to facilitate change for a user. In MI, there are five strategies that are useful in helping motivate change.

1. Introduce the topic with openness, concern, and lack of judgment to establish rapport

Establishing rapport with the user decreases defensiveness and increases openness to the possibility of change. Expressing acceptance and affirmation is important (Rollnick & Miller 1995).

> **Helper:** There are some signs of drug use and, because I care about your health, I'd like to explore ways I can help you. What can you tell me about your drug use?

2. Assess motivation

One method of assessing motivation is to use a scale of 1 to 10 and to ask why motivation is not *lower*:

>**Helper:** "How ready are you to quit, on a scale of 1 to 10?"
>**User:** "I'd say a 4.
>**Helper:** Why not lower?"
>**User:** "Lower? . . . Why not lower? Um, well, there's my job that's important to me . . ." (Asking, "Why not *lower*?" is likely to produce some statement of motivation, whereas asking, "Why not *higher*?" is likely to produce excuses.) Also, gauge the user's confidence in his/her ability to change and readiness for change (Rounsaville 2002).

3. Elicit statements of motivation

Use open-ended questioning and reflective listening to elicit the person's own explanations for behaviors, recognition or concerns about a problem, and desire, intention, and ability to change.

For example, say:

>**Helper:** "How is your drinking affecting your life?"
>**User:** "It's ruining my marriage!"

4. Resolve ambivalence

People in addiction often have a high degree of ambivalence about changing their addictive behavior (Wagner & Conners 2003c); they want both the pleasures of indulgence and the benefits of restraint. Help the person explore, articulate, and clarify ambivalence he or she may have about the problem behavior. Highlight discrepancies in what the person says in order to produce internal tension that can lead to change.

For example, say:

>**Helper:** "From what you say, drinking is important to your social life. while at the same time, it is hurting your most important relationships. What do you think about that?"
>**User:** "Keeping my girlfriend is really more important."

5. Plan for change

In motivational interviewing, the client comes up with his or her own plan for change (Ingersoll et al. 2000; Rosengren & Wagner 2001). Elicit a plan from the person for the next 30 to 90 days. The plan is based on the person's current stage of change and does not need to include quitting if he or she isn't ready.

For example, ask:

> **Helper:** "What step, if any, can you take in the next month to move in the direction of thinking about quitting?"
> **User:** "I can attend a follow-up appointment."

Here are the 12 Steps as defined by Alcoholics Anonymous:

1. We admitted we were powerless over alcohol–that our lives had become unmanageable.
2. We came to believe that a Power greater than ourselves could restore us to sanity.
3. We made a decision to turn our will and our lives over to the care of God as we understood Him.
4. We made a searching and fearless moral inventory of ourselves.
5. We admitted to God, to ourselves, and to another human being the exact nature of our wrongs.
6. We were entirely ready to have God remove all these defects of character.
7. We humbly asked Him to remove our shortcomings.
8. We made a list of persons we had harmed, and became willing to make amends to them all.
9. We made direct amends to such people wherever possible, except when to do so would injure them or others.
10. We continued to take personal inventory and when we were wrong, promptly admitted it.
11. We sought through prayer and meditation to improve our conscious contact with God as we understood Him, praying only for knowledge of His will for us and the power to carry that out.
12. Having had a spiritual awakening as the result of these steps, we tried to carry this message to alcoholics and to practice these principles in all our affairs.

Process Questions:

1. What do you think is the key to making motivational interviewing effective?
2. What is the role of faith in recovery?

6.3c Research has shown that self-help groups such as Alcoholics Anonymous (AA) and the 12 Steps assist with long-term sobriety and recovery.

6.4 The Dad Plan

> rct 15 | rst 15 | est 15 | page 115
>
> **State:** *This section is one of the most important parts of the course where you put knowledge into action.*
>
> **Instruct:** *Answer the following questions to create your Dad Plan to not quit or give up, but to draw support from faith, family, and the community.*

Fathering Skill: I will become a better dad no matter how tough; I won't quit or give up, through community support of my faith, family, and community until my last breath and my eyes finally shut.

Remember to use SMART goals for your plan to turn your life around.

Instructions: Answer the following questions to create your Dad Plan to become a better dad.

1. What is my specific SMART (Specific, Measurable, Achievable, Realistic, Timetable) goal for growing in cultural awareness?
2. What can I do every day this week to grow more culturally aware?
3. When and where will I do this?
4. Who will hold me accountable?

7.0 References

Bowlby, J. (1969), *Attachment and loss, Vol. 1: Attachment.* New York: Basic Books.

Epstein, N., Bishop, D., & Baldwin, L. (1984). McMaster model of family functioning. In D. H. Olson, & P. M. Miller (Eds.), Family studies review year-book (Vol. 2). New Delhi: Sage Publications

Gould, T. J. (2010). Addiction and cognition, *Addiction Science Clinical Practice*, 5(2), 4-14.

Henriques, G. (2013). On making judgments and being judgmental: Eight dynamics to consider in making constructive judgments. Psychology Today. Retrieved from: https://www.psychologytoday.com/blog/theory-knowledge/201305/making-judgments-and-being-judgmental

Henriques, D. (2014). The Core Need. Psychology Today. Retrieved from https://www.psychologytoday.com/blog/theory-knowledge/201406/the-core-need

Hibel, James, "Cooperation And Competition In Family, Pseudo-Family And Peer Triads" (1981). *Child and Family Studies—Dissertations.* 54. https://surface.syr.edu/cfs_etd/54

National Association of Social Workers. (2008). *Code of ethics of the National Association of Social Workers.* Washington, DC: NASW Press.

Prentice, R. (2014). Teaching behavioral ethics. Journal of Legal Studies Education, 31(2), 325-365.

Van der Kolk, B. A. (2014). *The body keeps the score: Brain, mind, and body in the healing of trauma.* New York: VikingU.S. Census. (2015). American Indian and Alaska Native Heritage Month: November 2015. Retrieved from https://www.census.gov/newsroom/facts-for-features/2015/cb15-ff22.html

Rycus, J. S. (1998). The field guide to child welfare volume III: Child development and child welfare, Child Welfare League of America Press.

Genovese, E. (1976). "The Political Crisis of Social History: A Marxian Perspective", Journal of Social History, 10(2), 205–220.

Seligman, M. E., & Maier, S. F. (1967). Failure to escape traumatic shock. *Journal of Experimental Psychology, 74(1),* 1-9.

www.ingramcontent.com/pod-product-compliance
Lightning Source LLC
Chambersburg PA
CBHW081747100526
44592CB00015B/2330